SERVICE HANDGUNS:
A collectors' guide

SERVICE HANDGUNS:
A collectors' guide

Klaus-Peter König and Martin Hugo

Translated from the German by
Alex Vanags-Baginskis

B.T. Batsford Ltd. London

Translated from the book *Waggensammeln: die wichtigsten Pistolen und Revolver seit 1850* by Klaus-Peter König and Martin Hugo, published by Motorbuch-Verlag, Stuttgart. Copyright © Motorbuch-Verlag, Stuttgart 1983

This edition first published 1988

ISBN 0 7134 5580 2

Printed and bound in Great Britain by
Richard Clay Ltd, Chichester, Sussex
for the Publishers B.T. Batsford Ltd, 4 Fitzhardinge Street,
London W1H 0AH

CONTENTS

Foreword

The development of weapons for practical purposes is important in the history of the human race because it was their use and improvement that allowed human beings to assert themselves in an unfriendly environment in which humans fitted in far less than the animals who lived there. The more accomplished the weapons became, the better could the humans hunt their prey; the weapons also protected the rights of their owners in the face of the rights or claims of others – and so unfortunately also brought the possibility of armed conflict.

We human beings have lived, and are still living, in a world whose raw materials and borders are secured by force of arms, or are being staked out anew, often despite international law; we have always had to adapt to what the effects of weapons and the force of arms have left us in terms of free space. Nowadays, modern weapons of destruction in various arsenals are paid for by taxes and controlled by the State; they have little in common with the cherished rarities kept by individual collectors.

It is not surprising that each epoch has made great efforts to perfect its weapons and develop them to the highest possible degree, always combined with the ability to produce them in sufficiently large quantities. Each weapon, as with any other commodity, reflects therefore the technical level of an epoch and, in a historical context, represents part of a long development history.

The number of handguns, good or bad, developed to date is legion and nobody could claim to present a truly complete work on the subject with any real hope of success. Only a proportion of the weapons that have evolved over the years in response to military requirements, or in a spirit of technical invention or business acumen, can ever be shown, and that applies to this present work which attempts to display the handguns most widely sought by collectors.

Most of the work involved in compiling a pictorial book like this consists of photographing the selected weapons and their accessories, all of which first have to be traced and made available. The start is easy, because the 'usual' collector's guns can be found in practically every private collection; it is when one reaches the more unusual weapons that the difficulties appear. Not infrequently it was sheer chance that helped us to show the reader some of the really rare items. It was during this search that we also had the unfortunate experience of finding that some collectors fought shy of making their well-preserved items available for public display. Quite often, the need for personal safety played a role in this and we had to respect it.

Some difficulties were quite unexpected, as for instance in compiling a Table giving the most important data for each weapon. A lot of this could be taken from the existing literature, except that the external dimensions quite often showed considerable variations. Without describing the data published in other works as false we would like to state that all measurements and data in this book relate specifically to the weapon illustrated and that any differences due to possible variations between examples have not been taken into consideration. Each weapon was individually measured and weighed, and all millimetre figures have been rounded up or down according to the accepted norms.

However, the later chapter dealing with pertinent ammunition could not be compiled more completely than it has been because no hints of any kind could be found regarding many cartridges. Their measurements and ballistic data were taken from the excellent *Handbuch der Pistolen- und Revolverpatronen* (Handbook of Pistol- and Revolver Cartridges) by Erlmeier and Brandt, which is the most thorough work on the subject. In all cases where we had our own cartridges these were checked against data published in the above work without any inconsistencies being found. The reader is asked not to take it amiss if in most cases we have not given the weight of the bullet and the powder charge because in the case of the rarer cartridges this would have required some dismantling. All those who are collectors themselves will understand our desire to preserve the value of the collected object. The same applies to the unopened cartridge boxes or the old cartridges which were not polished before they were photographed and often look somewhat dirty in the picture.

The year of construction also proved a problem because here too there were numerous inconsistencies in the literature and it just would not do simply to give the most frequently quoted year. In many cases authors were inclined to set down the date of a more or less common alternative as a new, and therefore a different year of construction. We have taken the view that the date range of the basic design should be taken as the 'year of construction' because after all this design was kept throughout all improvements and alterations.

The choice of pictures deliberately avoids perspective views because we felt these would make clear comparisons of size difficult, if not impossible. The handguns reproduced in the following pages are shown directly from the side to allow, for example, detailed comparison between variants. Additional pictures show, as far as available, accessories such as holsters or reloading tools because such accessories really give a collection completeness.

This book is intended as an easy reference guide to collectors of widely different tastes; it also attempts to show items which, because of their rarity value, would probably be out of reach of the individual collector but which he should know about because they are an important link in the chain of development.

Note on the photographs

If a book, such as this, is predominantly a photographic work then I feel the authors responsible for it should be allowed to say a few fundamental words regarding the preparation and finish of the many pictures.

The basic aim in preparing what is predominantly a photographic book is to make every picture as true a likeness of the given weapon as possible. So far, so good – but in fact that would only be wholly feasible in an expensive colour reproduction, and even then much would depend on the colour transparencies supplied. Only at the photograph stage – assuming the use of correctly measured lighting and exposure – will the photographed weapon be seen as it was in fact set in front of the camera. Once the book is printed, certain unavoidable falsificiations take place. For instance, the typical blue of a Colt case hardening will seldom be reproduced exactly as it is, the colour ranging from a more brownish shade to a dark colour, a variation which is completely beyond the control of the photographer.

The black-and-white photographs used in this book attempt to depict the weapons as close to the original as practicable, a difficult undertaking when it is a matter of showing all the fine gradations of colour, mottled hardening and other metal shadings, quite apart from the beauty of the finely finished woodwork of the grips.

Taking all this into account, this kind of reproduction remains an experiment, where we simply have to accept the distortions gradually introduced along the way from the negative via the print, the printing film and finally the printed reproduction. Every object is three-dimensional and the reproduction of protruding and recessed parts of the weapons posed a special problem which could only be solved by special lighting. Only when all the shadows, lighter-coloured parts and reflections are clearly seen in a picture is a 'plastic' effect presented to the onlooker. The various weapons reacted completely differently to the same lighting from the same direction so that it was necessary to photograph each weapon lit from two different directions. Only by comparing the resulting prints could we see with which lighting angles the weapon in question showed its typical characteristics and was best depicted; such pairs of pictures were therefore prepared for each weapon. However, this created a new problem because with altered direction of lighting the same weapon would often display quite unexpected patterns of reflection. Sand-blasted or polished or burnished areas were relatively simple; much more difficult were the brushed areas which would never cease to give new puzzles. It was also surprising to note that metal hardening, hardly noticeable with the naked eye, such as in the area around the ejector slots of self-loading pistols, could be made visible in a photograph just by changing the direction of lighting. To an onlooker unfamiliar with this phenomenon this hardening would appear in the picture looking rather like faulty gun-metal burnishing, worn parts or even blotches of lubricant.

All weapons were photographed directly side on and not from an angle to avoid perspective pictures. True enough, perspective pictures have the undeniable advantage of showing more details of the weapons' upper side (at the expense of revealing less of the underside), but this kind of representation would not allow an exact comparison of size because here too it would be a matter of compromise. In print it would be impossible to depict each weapon in relation to its actual size; the Borchardt pistol would have occupied several pages if we had represented just the pocket pistols in their original size. On the other hand, if the Borchardt was shown across the measured page and all other weapons depicted to scale, pictures of the smaller weapons would have revealed too few details. In short, we could not show the reduction to scale but only indicate it approximately. However, with the aid of the mostly complete technical data it is quite possible to grasp the actual dimensions, or measure parts of the weapon in the picture in relation to the known over-all length – quite important when it is a matter of restoring an incomplete weapon with spare parts or checking restored parts as to their original size.

No attempt was made to 'improve' the weapons for photographic purposes despite the fact that such 'artistic touches' as blackening parts that were too shiny would have considerably eased our work. On the one hand, this would not have looked right in the picture and, on the other, some collectors would not have allowed us to carry out such operations on their guns, some of which were very valuable. Cases where the weapons have a 'signature' in white depict them in the condition as we found them and not necessarily as they would look originally. The additional display of the description and stamping with indelible white paint is a bad American habit not practised in Germany, not even by means of a temporary powdering of the (recessed) inscription. In any case, the inscription is often so clearly seen that this 'addition' is completely superfluous; these details are always listed separately in the respective Tables.

The pictures submitted for printing are completely 'natural', i.e. without any retouching or 'improvements' of any kind. After all, the weapon must be shown as it is; traces of its use or scratches are part of a collector's item that has a long and often troubled history behind it. Only in a very few cases was it necessary to 'touch up' some parts that had reproduced too brightly, but tese are exceptions.

How can a two-dimensional piece of paper give a true representation of a three-dimensional object? We trust that the sideviews and detail pictures reproduced in this book are the most faithful possible depictions of those items which you have chosen to collect or study out of your own personal interest.

Klaus-Peter König

AUSTRIA

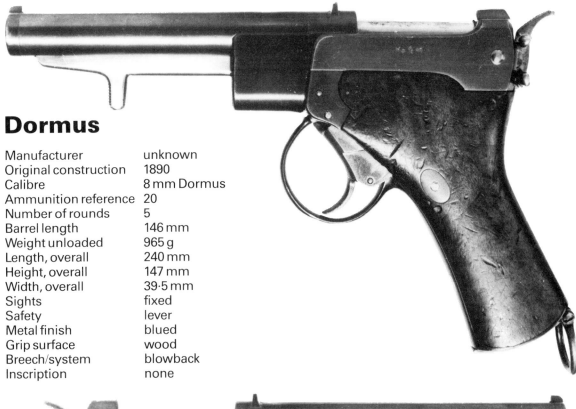

Dormus

Manufacturer	unknown
Original construction	1890
Calibre	8 mm Dormus
Ammunition reference	20
Number of rounds	5
Barrel length	146 mm
Weight unloaded	965 g
Length, overall	240 mm
Height, overall	147 mm
Width, overall	39·5 mm
Sights	fixed
Safety	lever
Metal finish	blued
Grip surface	wood
Breech/system	blowback
Inscription	none

Manufacturer	Rast u. Gasser, Vienna
Original construction	1898
Calibre	·22 LR
Ammunition reference	1
Number of rounds	8
Barrel length	116·1 mm
Weight unloaded	1040 g
Length, overall	223 mm
Height, overall	159 mm
Width, overall	40·3 mm
Sights	fixed
Safety	none
Metal finish	blued
Grip surface	wood
Breech/system	double-action
Inscription	PATENT
	RAST & GASSER
	WIEN

AUSTRIA Rast und Gasser Mod. 1898

Manufacturer	Rast u. Gasser, Vienna
Original construction	1898
Calibre	8 mm Gasser
Ammunition reference	25
Number of rounds	8
Barrel length	106·4 mm
Weight unloaded	955 g
Length, overall	225 mm
Height, overall	159 mm
Width, overall	41 mm
Sights	fixed
Safety	none
Metal finish	blued
Grip surface	wood
Breech/system	double-action
Inscription	PATENT
	RAST & GASSER
	WIEN

Manufacturer	Oesterr. Waffenfabriks-gesellschaft, Steyr (Austrian Arms Factory Company
Original construction	1895
Calibre	8 mm Steyr
Ammunition reference	27
Number of rounds	10
Barrel length	127 mm
Weight unloaded	1005 g
Length, overall	233 mm
Height, overall	160 mm
Width, overall	32·8 mm
Sights	fixed
Safety	none
Metal finish	blued
Grip surface	wood
Breech/system	locked
Inscription	WAFFENFABRIK STEYR

Manufacturer	Fegyvergyar-Budapest
Original construction	1895
Calibre	8 mm Steyr
Ammunition reference	27
Number of rounds	10
Barrel length	128·3 mm
Weight unloaded	1015 g
Length, overall	232·5 mm
Height, overall	159 mm
Width, overall	33 mm
Sights	fixed
Safety	none
Metal finish	blued
Grip surface	wood
Breech/system	locked
Inscription	FEGYVERGYAR-BUDAPEST

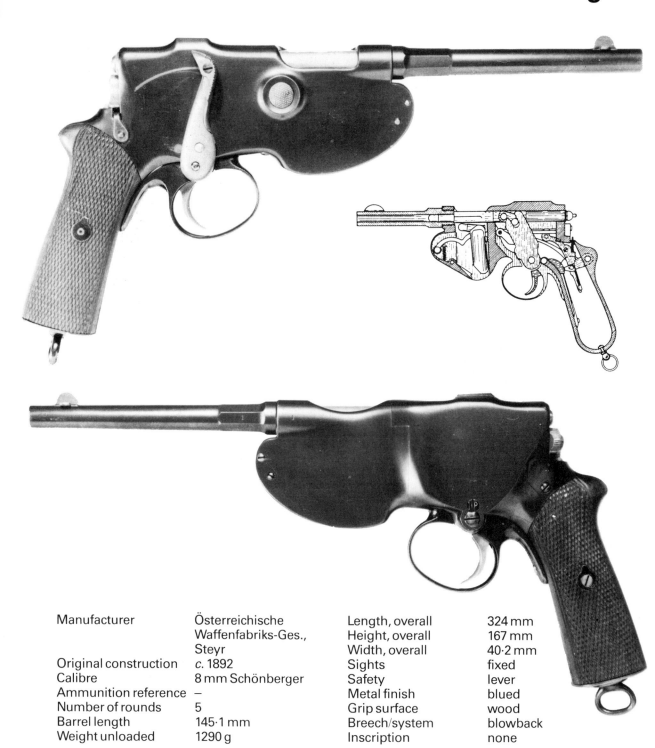

Manufacturer	Österreichische Waffenfabriks-Ges., Steyr	Length, overall	324 mm
		Height, overall	167 mm
		Width, overall	40·2 mm
Original construction	c. 1892	Sights	fixed
Calibre	8 mm Schönberger	Safety	lever
Ammunition reference	–	Metal finish	blued
Number of rounds	5	Grip surface	wood
Barrel length	145·1 mm	Breech/system	blowback
Weight unloaded	1290 g	Inscription	none

Manufacturer	Österreichische Waffenfabriks-Ges., Steyr
Original construction	1908
Calibre	7·65 mm Browning
Ammunition reference	17
Number of rounds	6
Barrel length	90 mm
Weight unloaded	630 g
Length, overall	164 mm
Height, overall	109 mm
Width, overall	30 mm
Sights	fixed
Safety	lever
Metal finish	blued
Grip surface	vulcanized rubber
Breech/system	blow-back
Inscription	OESTERR. WAFFEN-FABRIKS-GES. STEYR PAT. No. 25025-06 U. No. 16715-08 N. PIEPER PATENT PAT. No. 40335

Manufacturer	Österreichische Waffenfabriksgesellschaft, Steyr
Original construction	1909
Calibre	7·65 mm Browning
Ammunition reference	17
Number of rounds	7
Barrel length	90 mm
Weight unloaded	690 g
Length, overall	168 mm
Height, overall	118 mm
Width, overall	28 mm
Sights	fixed
Safety	lever
Metal finish	blued
Grip surface	vulcanized rubber
Breech/system	blowback
Inscription	Pat. No. 9379-05 u. No. 25025-06 Pat. No. 40335

Steyr Mod. 1911 (Chile)

Manufacturer	Österreichische Waffenfabriksgesellschaft, Steyr
Original construction	1911
Calibre	9 mm Steyr
Ammunition reference	37
Number of rounds	8
Barrel length	129·5 mm
Weight unloaded	985 g
Length, overall	217 mm
Height, overall	143 mm
Width, overall	30·2 mm
Sights	fixed
Safety	lever
Metal finish	blued
Grip surface	wood
Breech/system	locked
Inscription	STEYR 1912 MOD. 1911 EJERCITO DE CHILE FUERZA AEREA DE CHILE

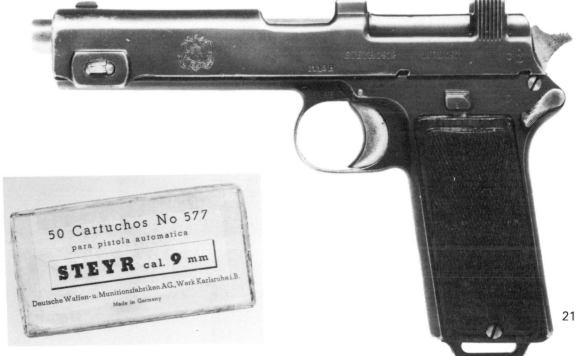

50 Cartuchos No 577
para pistola automatica
STEYR cal. 9 mm
Deutsche Waffen- u. Munitionsfabriken AG., Werk Karlsruhe i. B.
Made in Germany

Manufacturer	Österreichische Waffenfabriksgesellschaft, Steyr
Original construction	1911
Calibre	9 mm Steyr
Ammunition reference	37
Number of rounds	8
Barrel length	129·1 mm
Weight unloaded	965 g
Length, overall	217 mm
Height, overall	143 mm
Width, overall	30·8 mm
Sights	fixed
Safety	lever
Metal finish	blued
Grip surface	wood
Breech/system	locked
Inscription	STEYR 1914

AUSTRIA

Steyr Mod. 12/16

Manufacturer	Österreichische Waffenfabriksgesellschaft, Steyr
Original construction	1911
Calibre	9 mm Steyr
Ammunition reference	37
Number of rounds	16
Barrel length	129·8 mm
Weight unloaded	1095 g
Length, overall	217 mm
Height, overall	232 mm
Width, overall	30·6 mm
Sights	fixed
Safety	lever
Metal finish	blued
Grip surface	wood
Breech/system	locked
Inscription	STEYR 1919

Manufacturer	Österreichische Waffenfabriksgesellschaft, Steyr
Original construction	1911
Calibre	9 mm Para
Ammunition reference	34
Number of rounds	8
Barrel length	130 mm
Weight unloaded	960 g
Length, overall	216 mm
Height, overall	143 mm
Width, overall	30·2 mm
Sights	fixed
Safety	lever
Metal finish	blued
Grip surface	wood
Breech/system	locked
Inscription	STEYR 1919 08

Manufacturer	Österreichische Waffenfabriksgesellschaft, Steyr
Original construction	1911
Calibre	9 mm Para
Ammunition reference	34
Number of rounds	8
Barrel length	129·8 mm
Weight unloaded	960 g
Length, overall	217 mm
Height, overall	143 mm
Width, overall	30 mm
Sights	fixed
Safety	lever
Metal finish	blued
Grip surface	wood
Breech/system	locked
Inscription	Steyr 1915 08

BELGIUM

Bergmann Mars

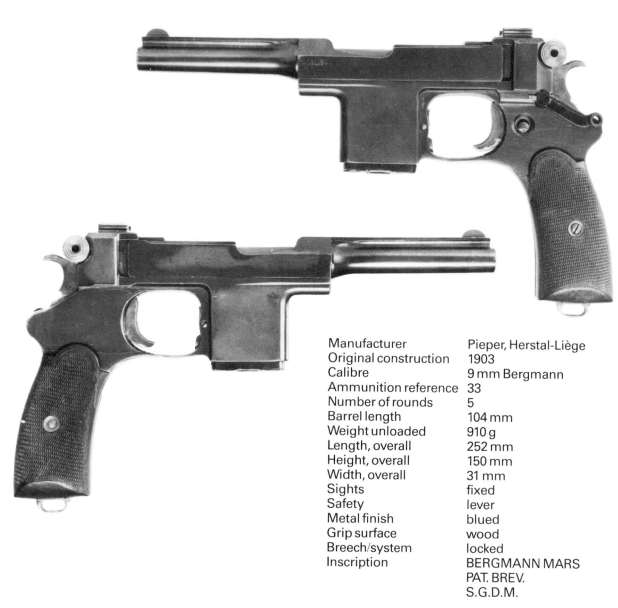

Manufacturer	Pieper, Herstal-Liège
Original construction	1903
Calibre	9 mm Bergmann
Ammunition reference	33
Number of rounds	5
Barrel length	104 mm
Weight unloaded	910 g
Length, overall	252 mm
Height, overall	150 mm
Width, overall	31 mm
Sights	fixed
Safety	lever
Metal finish	blued
Grip surface	wood
Breech/system	locked
Inscription	BERGMANN MARS PAT. BREV. S.G.D.M.

Bergmann Simplex

Manufacturer	unknown
Original construction	1902
Calibre	8 mm Simplex
Ammunition reference	22
Number of rounds	5
Barrel length	71·5 mm
Weight unloaded	625 g
Length, overall	193 mm
Height, overall	119 mm
Width, overall	32·5 mm
Sights	fixed
Safety	lever
Metal finish	blued
Grip surface	vulcanized rubber
Breech/system	locked
Inscription	PATENT
	BREVETE
	S.G.D.M.

BELGIUM

FN Mod. 1900

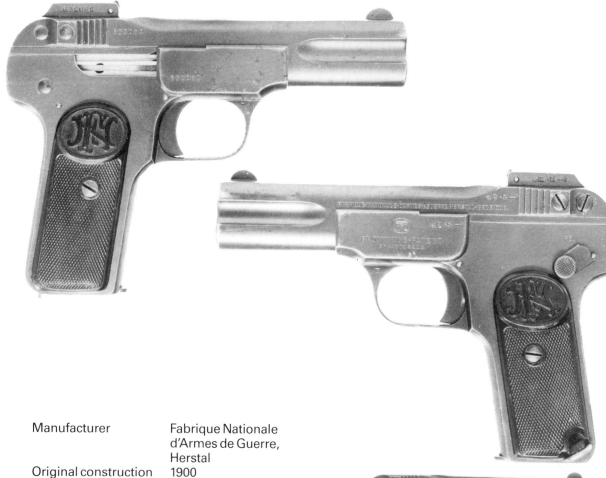

Manufacturer	Fabrique Nationale d'Armes de Guerre, Herstal
Original construction	1900
Calibre	7·65 mm Browning
Ammunition reference	17
Number of rounds	7
Barrel length	101·9 mm
Weight unloaded	630 g
Length, overall	164 mm
Height, overall	117 mm
Width, overall	32·6 mm
Sights	fixed
Safety	lever
Metal finish	blued
Grip surface	vulcanized rubber
Breech/system	blowback
Inscription	FABRIQUE-NATIONALE-HERSTAL-LIEGE (BROWNING'S-PATENT) BREVETE-S.G.D.M.

Manufacturer	Fabrique Nationale d'Armes de Guerre, Herstal
Original construction	1900
Calibre	7·65 mm Browning
Ammunition reference	17
Number of rounds	7
Barrel length	102 mm
Weight unloaded	640 g
Length, overall	163 mm
Height, overall	116 mm
Width, overall	29·3 mm
Sights	fixed
Safety	lever
Metal finish	blued
Grip surface	vulcanized rubber
Breech/system	blowback
Inscription	FABRIQUE NATIONALE D'ARMES DE GUERRE HERSTAL BELGIQUE BROWNINGS PATENT BREVETE S.G.D.G.

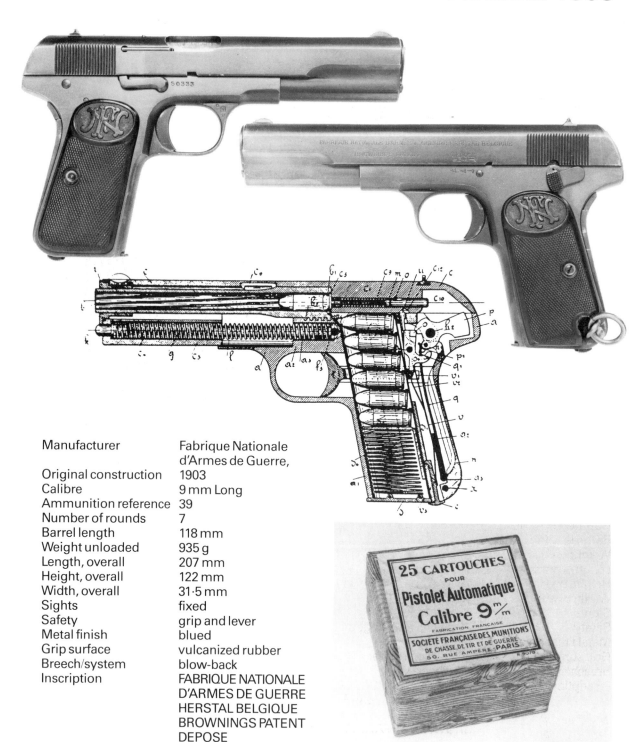

Manufacturer	Fabrique Nationale d'Armes de Guerre,
Original construction	1903
Calibre	9 mm Long
Ammunition reference	39
Number of rounds	7
Barrel length	118 mm
Weight unloaded	935 g
Length, overall	207 mm
Height, overall	122 mm
Width, overall	31·5 mm
Sights	fixed
Safety	grip and lever
Metal finish	blued
Grip surface	vulcanized rubber
Breech/system	blow-back
Inscription	FABRIQUE NATIONALE D'ARMES DE GUERRE HERSTAL BELGIQUE BROWNINGS PATENT DEPOSE

25 CARTOUCHES
POUR
Pistolet Automatique
Calibre 9 m/m
FABRICATION FRANÇAISE
SOCIÉTÉ FRANÇAISE DES MUNITIONS
DE CHASSE DE TIR ET DE GUERRE
50. RUE AMPERE · PARIS

BELGIUM

FN Mod. 1906

Manufacturer	Fabrique Nationale d'Armes de Guerre, Herstal
Original construction	1906
Calibre	6·35 mm Browning
Ammunition reference	3
Number of rounds	6
Barrel length	53·4 mm
Weight unloaded	370 g
Length, overall	115 mm
Height, overall	79 mm
Width, overall	23·4 mm
Sights	fixed
Safety	lever, grip and magazine
Metal finish	blued
Grip surface	vulcanized rubber
Breech/system	blowback
Inscription	FABRIQUE NATIONALE D'ARMES DE GUERRE HERSTAL BELGIQUE BROWNINGS PATENT DEPOSE

Manufacturer	Fabrique Nationale d'Armes de Guerre, Herstal		
Original construction	1910		
Calibre	9 mm Browning		
Ammunition reference	35		
Number of rounds	6		
Barrel length	87·5 mm		
Weight unloaded	570 g		
Length, overall	153 mm		
Height, overall	100 mm		
Width, overall	27 mm		
Sights	fixed	Inscription	FABRIQUE NATIONALE D'ARMES DE GUERRE HERSTAL BELGIQUE BROWNINGS PATENT DEPOSE
Safety	lever, magazine and grip		
Metal finish	blued		
Grip surface	vulcanized rubber		
Breech/system	blowback		

Manufacturer	Fabrique Nationale d'Armes de Guerre, Herstal
Original construction	1910
Calibre	9 mm Browning
Ammunition reference	35
Number of rounds	8
Barrel length	112·8 mm
Weight unloaded	685 g
Length, overall	179 mm
Height, overall	121 mm
Width, overall	32·6 mm
Sights	fixed
Safety	lever and grip
Metal finish	blued
Grip surface	hardened
Breech/system	blowback
Inscription	FABRIQUE NATIONALE D'ARMES DE GUERRE HERSTAL BELGIQUE BROWNINGS PATENT DEPOSE

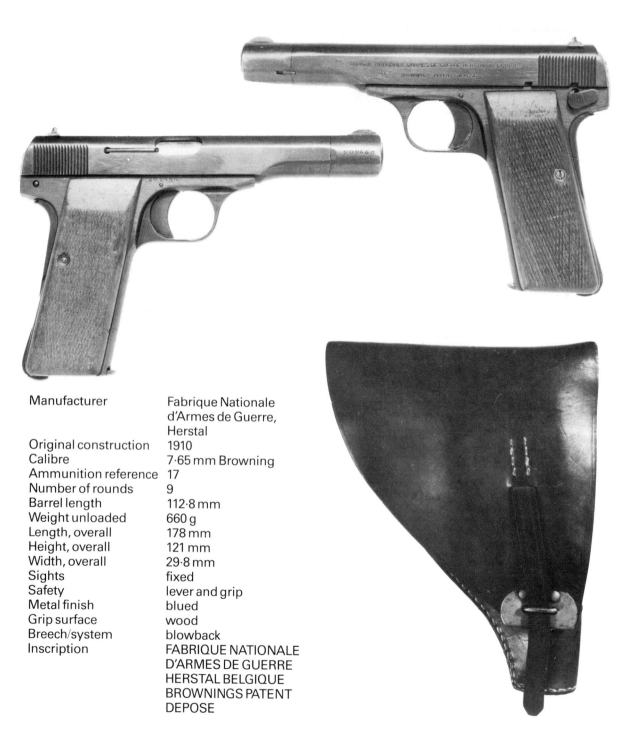

Manufacturer	Fabrique Nationale d'Armes de Guerre, Herstal
Original construction	1910
Calibre	7·65 mm Browning
Ammunition reference	17
Number of rounds	9
Barrel length	112·8 mm
Weight unloaded	660 g
Length, overall	178 mm
Height, overall	121 mm
Width, overall	29·8 mm
Sights	fixed
Safety	lever and grip
Metal finish	blued
Grip surface	wood
Breech/system	blowback
Inscription	FABRIQUE NATIONALE D'ARMES DE GUERRE HERSTAL BELGIQUE BROWNINGS PATENT DEPOSE

Manufacturer	Fabrique Nationale d'Armes de Guerre, Herstal
Original construction	1927/28
Calibre	9 mm Para
Ammunition reference	34
Number of rounds	13
Barrel length	120 mm
Weight unloaded	910 g
Length, overall	218 mm
Height, overall	136 mm
Width, overall	35 mm
Sights	0-500 m
Safety	lever and magazine
Metal finish	blued
Grip surface	wood
Breech/system	locked
Inscription	FABRIQUE NATIONALE D'ARMES DE GUERRE HERSTAL BELGIQUE BROWNINGS PATENT DEPOSE

Manufacturer	Fabrique Nationale d'Armes de Guerre, Herstal
Original construction	1927/28
Calibre	9 mm Para
Ammunition reference	34
Number of rounds	13
Barrel length	118·5 mm
Weight unloaded	915 g
Length, overall	197 mm
Height, overall	129 mm
Width, overall	35·3 mm
Sights	fixed
Safety	lever and magazine
Metal finish	blued
Grip surface	wood
Breech/system	locked
Inscription	FABRIQUE NATIONALE D'ARMES DE GUERRE HERSTAL BELGIQUE BROWNINGS PATENT DEPOSE

BELGIUM

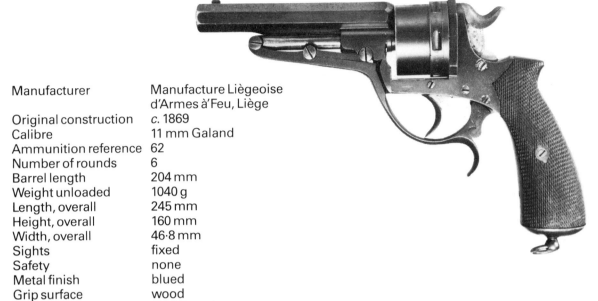

Manufacturer	Manufacture Liègeoise d'Armes à'Feu, Liège
Original construction	*c.* 1869
Calibre	11 mm Galand
Ammunition reference	62
Number of rounds	6
Barrel length	204 mm
Weight unloaded	1040 g
Length, overall	245 mm
Height, overall	160 mm
Width, overall	46·8 mm
Sights	fixed
Safety	none
Metal finish	blued
Grip surface	wood
Breech/system	double action
Inscription	none

BELGIUM

Galand

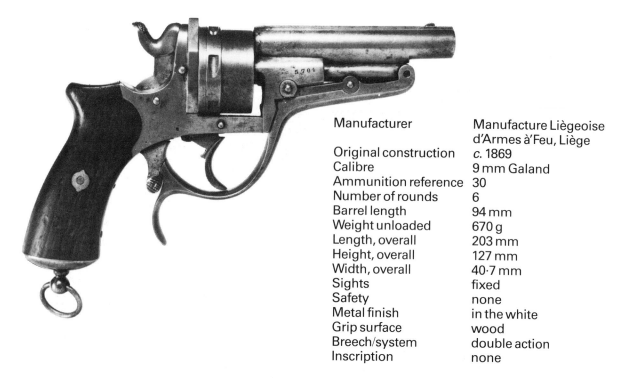

Manufacturer	Manufacture Liègeoise d'Armes à'Feu, Liège
Original construction	*c.* 1869
Calibre	9 mm Galand
Ammunition reference	30
Number of rounds	6
Barrel length	94 mm
Weight unloaded	670 g
Length, overall	203 mm
Height, overall	127 mm
Width, overall	40·7 mm
Sights	fixed
Safety	none
Metal finish	in the white
Grip surface	wood
Breech/system	double action
Inscription	none

Manufacturer	Nagant, Lüttich
Original construction	1887
Calibre	7·5 mm Swedish Ordnance (Nagant)
Ammunition reference	7
Number of rounds	6
Barrel length	114·2 mm
Weight unloaded	790 g
Length, overall	235 mm
Height, overall	145 mm
Width, overall	37·8 mm
Sights	fixed
Safety	none
Metal finish	blued
Grip surface	wood
Breech/system	double action
Inscription	BREVETE NAGANT

Bergmann Bayard Mod. 1910

Manufacturer	Pieper, Herstal-Liège
Original construction	1903
Calibre	9 mm Bergmann-Bayard
Ammunition reference	33
Number of rounds	6
Barrel length	101·6 mm
Weight unloaded	1010 g
Length, overall	253 mm
Height, overall	142 mm
Width, overall	35·5 mm
Sights	fixed
Safety	lever
Metal finish	blued
Grip surface	wood
Breech/system	locked
Inscription	ANCIENS ETABLISSE-MENTS PIEPER HERSTAL-LIEGE BERGMANN'S PATENT BREVETE S.G.D.M.

BELGIUM   Bergmann-Bayard Mod. 1910/21

Manufacturer	Pieper, Herstal-Liège
Original construction	1903
Calibre	9 mm Bergmann-Bayard
Ammunition reference	33
Number of rounds	6
Barrel length	101 mm
Weight unloaded	1090 g
Length, overall	253 mm
Height, overall	141 mm
Width, overall	38·5 mm
Sights	fixed
Safety	lever
Metal finish	blued
Grip surface	vulcanized
Breech/system	locked
Inscription	ANCIENS ETABLISSE-MENTS PIEPER HERSTAL-LIEGE BERGMANN'S PATENT BREVETE S.G.D.M.

CANADA

FN HP Mod. 35 Inglis Canada

Manufacturer	John Inglis, Canada
Original construction	1927/28
Calibre	9 mm Para
Ammunition reference	34
Number of rounds	13
Barrel length	118·5 mm
Weight unloaded	960 g
Length, overall	197 mm
Height, overall	132 mm
Width, overall	35·6 mm
Sights	fixed
Safety	lever and magazine
Metal finish	Parkerised
Grip surface	vulcanized rubber
Breech/system	locked
Inscription	BROWNING-FN 9 MM HP INGLIS CANADA MK I*

FN HP Mod. 35 Inglis Canada

Manufacturer	John Inglis, Canada
Original construction	1927/28
Calibre	9 mm Para
Ammunition reference	34
Number of rounds	13
Barrel length	118·5 mm
Weight unloaded	970 g
Length, overall	198 mm
Height, overall	132 mm
Width, overall	35·3 mm
Sights	fixed
Safety	lever and magazine
Metal finish	lacquered
Grip surface	vulcanized rubber
Breech/system	locked
Inscription	BROWNING-FN 9 MM HP
	INGLIS CANADA
	MK I*

CZECHOSLOVAKIA

CZ Mod. 27

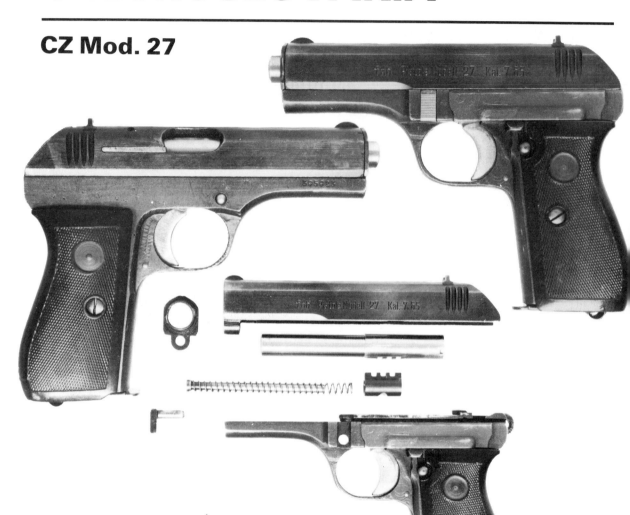

Manufacturer	Böhmische Waffenfabrik AG, Prague*
Original construction	1927
Calibre	7·65 mm Browning
Ammunition reference	17
Number of rounds	8
Barrel length	99·4 mm
Weight unloaded	715 g
Length, overall	160 mm
Height, overall	124 mm
Width, overall	27·4 mm

Sights	fixed
Safety	lever and magazine
Metal finish	blued
Grip surface	vulcanized rubber
Breech/system	blow-back
Inscription	fnh Pistole Modell 27 Kal. 7, 65

*This name used during production for German armed forces under the occupation 1938-44; original name : Ceska Zbrojovka, Prag. *Tr.*

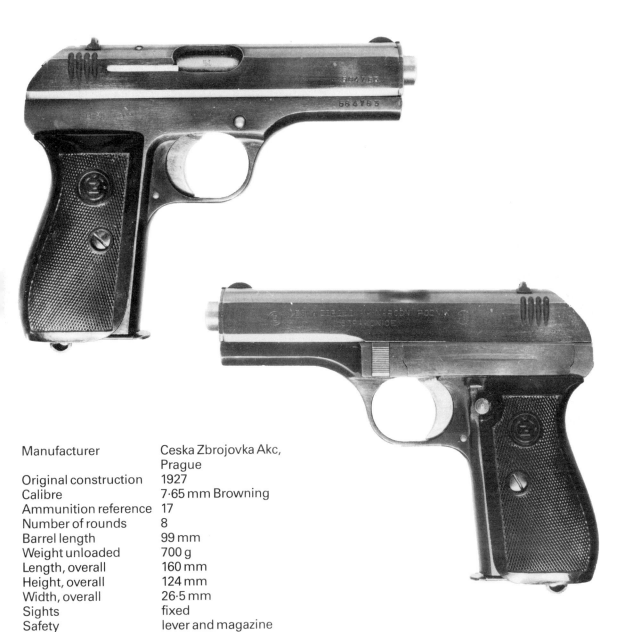

Manufacturer	Ceska Zbrojovka Akc, Prague
Original construction	1927
Calibre	7·65 mm Browning
Ammunition reference	17
Number of rounds	8
Barrel length	99 mm
Weight unloaded	700 g
Length, overall	160 mm
Height, overall	124 mm
Width, overall	26·5 mm
Sights	fixed
Safety	lever and magazine
Metal finish	blued
Grip surface	vulcanized rubber
Breech/system	blow-back
Inscription	CESKA ZBROJOVKA-NARODNI PODNIK STRAKONICE NB 49

CZECHOSLOVAKIA CZ Mod. 1938

Manufacturer	Ceska Zbrojovka Akc, Prague
Original construction	1937
Calibre	9 mm Browning
Ammunition reference	35
Number of rounds	8
Barrel length	119·5 mm
Weight unloaded	915 g
Length, overall	196 mm
Height, overall	142 mm
Width, overall	27·6 mm
Sights	fixed
Safety	none
Metal finish	blued
Grip surface	vulcanized rubber
Breech/system	blowback
Inscription	CESKA ZBROJOVKA-AKC. SPAL V PRAZE

CZECHOSLOVAKIA
CZ Mod. 52

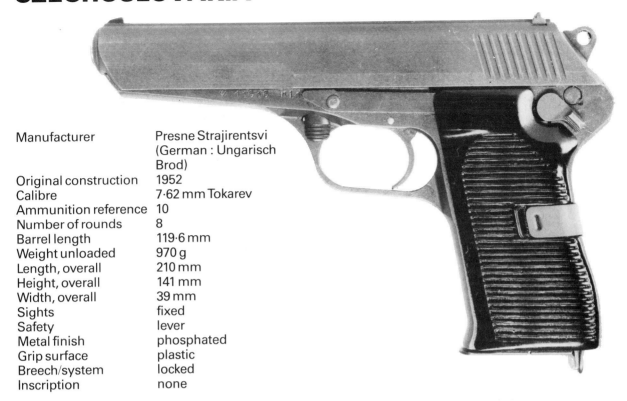

Manufacturer	Presne Strajirentsvi (German : Ungarisch Brod)
Original construction	1952
Calibre	7·62 mm Tokarev
Ammunition reference	10
Number of rounds	8
Barrel length	119·6 mm
Weight unloaded	970 g
Length, overall	210 mm
Height, overall	141 mm
Width, overall	39 mm
Sights	fixed
Safety	lever
Metal finish	phosphated
Grip surface	plastic
Breech/system	locked
Inscription	none

DENMARK

Bergmann Bayard Mod. 1910/21

Manufacturer	Haerens Rustkammer
Original construction	1903/8
Calibre	9 mm Bergmann-Bayard
Ammunition reference	35
Number of rounds	6
Barrel length	100·4 mm
Weight unloaded	1035 g
Length, overall	253 mm
Height, overall	142 mm
Width, overall	39·3 mm
Sights	fixed
Safety	lever
Metal finish	blued
Grip surface	wood
Breech/system	locked
Inscription	HAERENS RUSTKAMMER 19^{10}/$_{21}$

DENMARK   Schouboe

Manufacturer	Dansk Rekylriffel Syndikat, Copenhagen
Original construction	1907
Calibre	11·35 mm Schouboe
Ammunition reference	51
Number of rounds	7
Barrel length	129 mm
Weight unloaded	1015 g
Length, overall	228 mm
Height, overall	139 mm
Width, overall	32 mm
Sights	fixed
Safety	lever
Metal finish	blued
Grip surface	sheet metal
Breech/system	blowback
Inscription	Dansk-Rekylriffel-Syndikat KØBENHAVN

DENMARK   Schouboe

Manufacturer	Dansk Rekylriffel Syndikat, Copenhagen
Original construction	1907
Calibre	11·35 mm Schouboe
Ammunition reference	51
Number of rounds	7
Barrel length	128·5 mm
Weight unloaded	1110 g
Length, overall	225 mm
Height, overall	136 mm
Width, overall	34·7 mm
Sights	fixed
Safety	lever
Metal finish	blued
Grip surface	wood
Breech/system	blowback
Inscription	DANSK-REKYLRIFFEL-SYNDIKAT KØBENHAVN PATENT SCHOUBOE

FRANCE

French Army Revolver Mod. 1873

Manufacturer	Manufacture d'Armes St. Etienne
Original construction	1873
Calibre	11 mm French Ordnance
Ammunition reference	49 (48)
Number of rounds	6
Barrel length	115·3 mm
Weight unloaded	1145 g
Length, overall	240 mm
Height, overall	151 mm
Width, overall	45·1 mm
Sights	fixed
Safety	none
Metal finish	in the white
Grip surface	wood
Breech/system	double action
Inscription	*Mle d'Armes Mle 1873 St Etienne S. 1880*

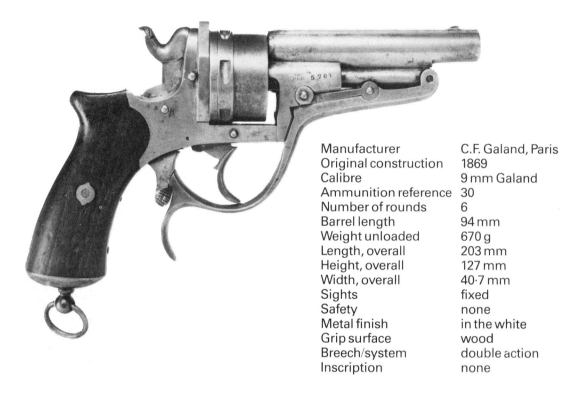

Manufacturer	C.F. Galand, Paris
Original construction	1869
Calibre	9 mm Galand
Ammunition reference	30
Number of rounds	6
Barrel length	94 mm
Weight unloaded	670 g
Length, overall	203 mm
Height, overall	127 mm
Width, overall	40·7 mm
Sights	fixed
Safety	none
Metal finish	in the white
Grip surface	wood
Breech/system	double action
Inscription	none

Manufacturer	C.F. Galand, Paris
Original construction	c. 1869
Calibre	11 mm Galand
Ammunition reference	62
Number of rounds	6
Barrel length	126 mm
Weight unloaded	1370 g
Length, overall	331 mm
Height, overall	145 mm
Width, overall	53 mm
Sights	fixed
Safety	none
Metal finish	blued
Grip surface	wood
Breech/system	double action
Inscription	GALAND PARIS

FRANCE

Galand

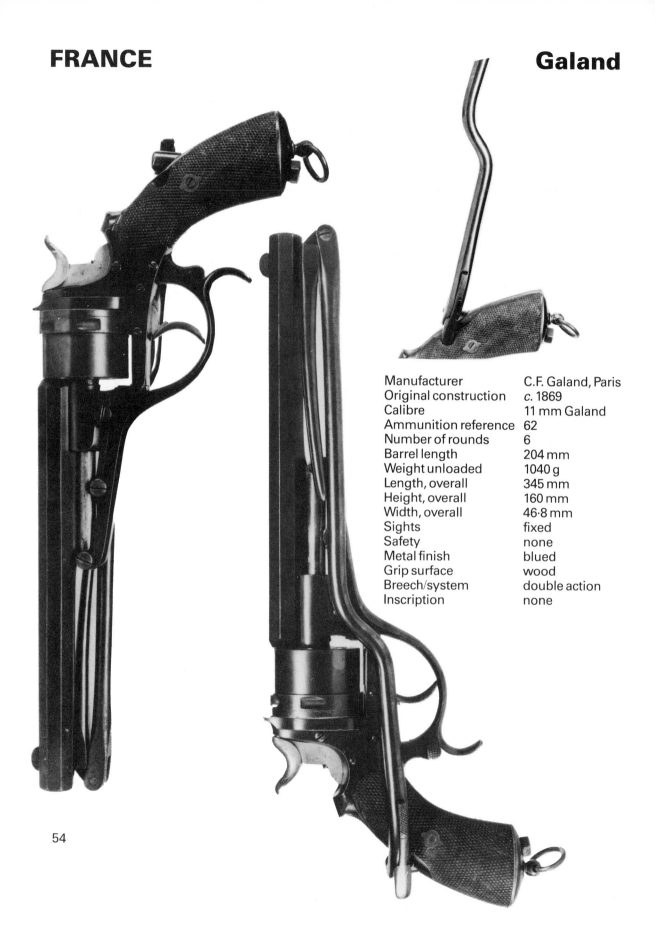

Manufacturer	C.F. Galand, Paris
Original construction	*c.* 1869
Calibre	11 mm Galand
Ammunition reference	62
Number of rounds	6
Barrel length	204 mm
Weight unloaded	1040 g
Length, overall	345 mm
Height, overall	160 mm
Width, overall	46·8 mm
Sights	fixed
Safety	none
Metal finish	blued
Grip surface	wood
Breech/system	double action
Inscription	none

FRANCE Lebel Revolver 1892

Manufacturer	Manufacture d'Armes, St. Etienne
Original construction	1892
Calibre	8 mm Lebel
Ammunition reference	24
Number of rounds	6
Barrel length	116·5 mm
Weight unloaded	840 g
Length, overall	237 mm
Height, overall	156 mm
Width, overall	38·8 mm
Sights	fixed
Safety	none
Metal finish	blackened
Grip surface	wood
Breech/system	double action
Inscription	*Mle. d'Armes St. Etienne S. 1914*

S.F.M. 2-40
6 CARTOUCHES
P. REVOLVER Mle 1892
CHARGE 0.25 Tr
LOT 55
R.9062

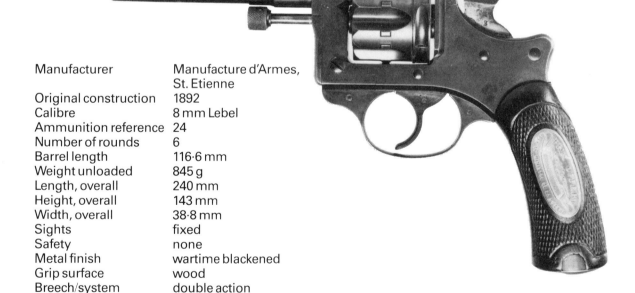

Manufacturer	Manufacture d'Armes, St. Etienne
Original construction	1892
Calibre	8 mm Lebel
Ammunition reference	24
Number of rounds	6
Barrel length	116·6 mm
Weight unloaded	845 g
Length, overall	240 mm
Height, overall	143 mm
Width, overall	38·8 mm
Sights	fixed
Safety	none
Metal finish	wartime blackened
Grip surface	wood
Breech/system	double action
Inscription	*Mle. d'Armes St. Etienne*

FRANCE

Le Français

Manufacturer	Manufacture d'Armes, St. Etienne
Original construction	1931
Calibre	7·65 mm Browning
Ammunition reference	17
Number of rounds	7
Barrel length	83 mm
Weight unloaded	650 g
Length, overall	153 mm
Height, overall	122 mm
Width, overall	29·3 mm
Sights	fixed
Safety	none
Metal finish	blued
Grip surface	vulcanized rubber
Breech/system	blowback
Inscription	LE FRANCAIS CAL. 7, 65 MANUFRANCE SAINT-ETIENNE

FRANCE

Le Français

Manufacturer	Manufacture d'Armes, St. Etienne
Original construction	1931
Calibre	9 mm Largo
Ammunition reference	33
Number of rounds	8
Barrel length	127·6 mm
Weight unloaded	965 g
Length, overall	203 mm
Height, overall	143 mm
Width, overall	33·7 mm
Sights	fixed
Safety	none
Metal finish	blued
Grip surface	wood
Breech/system	blowback
Inscription	MAS D'ARMES ET CYCLES DE SAINT-ETIENNE FABRICATION FRANCAISE

FRANCE

Le Français

Manufacturer	Manufacture d'Armes, St. Etienne
Original construction	1931
Calibre	9 mm Largo
Ammunition reference	33
Number of rounds	8
Barrel length	128·1 mm
Weight unloaded	1060 g
Length, overall	203 mm
Height, overall	135 mm
Width, overall	33·6 mm
Sights	fixed
Safety	none
Metal finish	blued
Grip surface	vulcanized rubber
Breech/system	blowback
Inscription	TYPE ARMEE MANUFACTURE FRANCAISE D'ARMES ET CYCLES DE SAINT-ETIENNE

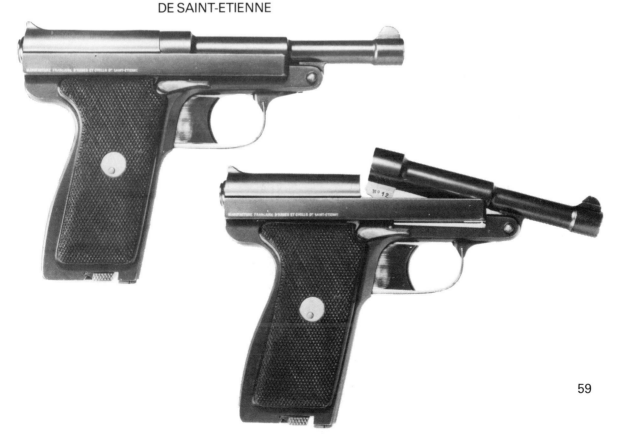

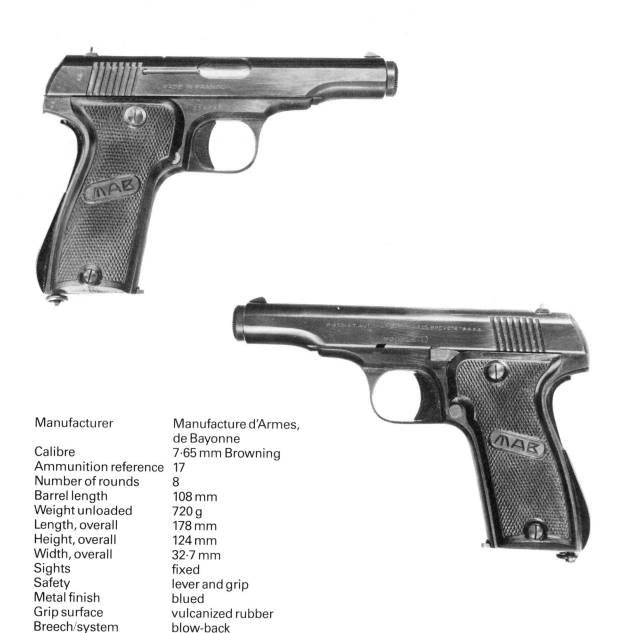

Manufacturer	Manufacture d'Armes, de Bayonne
Calibre	7·65 mm Browning
Ammunition reference	17
Number of rounds	8
Barrel length	108 mm
Weight unloaded	720 g
Length, overall	178 mm
Height, overall	124 mm
Width, overall	32·7 mm
Sights	fixed
Safety	lever and grip
Metal finish	blued
Grip surface	vulcanized rubber
Breech/system	blow-back
Inscription	PISTOLET AUTOMATIQUE MAB BREVETE S.G.D.G. MODELE D MADE IN FRANCE

FRANCE

Petter Mod. 1935A

Manufacturer	Société Alsacienne de Constructions Mécaniques	Height, overall	126 mm
Original construction	1935	Width, overall	29·8 mm
Calibre	7·65 mm Long	Sights	fixed
Ammunition reference	18	Safety	lever and magazine
Number of rounds	8	Metal finish	lacquered
Barrel length	120·1 mm	Grip surface	vulcanized rubber
Weight unloaded	750 g	Breech/system	locked
Length, overall	196 mm	Inscription	MI^e 1935 A S.A.C.M.

FRANCE

Petter Mod. 1935 S

Manufacturer	Manufacture d'Armes Chatellerault
Original construction	1935
Calibre	7·65 mm Long
Ammunition reference	18
Number of rounds	8
Barrel length	105·6 mm
Weight unloaded	770 g
Length, overall	188 mm
Height, overall	121 mm
Width, overall	28·5 mm
Sights	fixed
Safety	lever and magazine
Metal finish	blued
Grip surface	vulcanized rubber
Breech/system	locked
Inscription	MODELE 1935 S
	MAC-B
	CAL. 7, 65 L
	MAC

FRANCE

Petter M 50

Manufacturer	Manufacture d'Armes Chatellerault
Original construction	1950
Calibre	9 mm Para
Ammunition reference	34
Number of rounds	8
Barrel length	110·7 mm
Weight unloaded	975 g
Length, overall	194 mm
Height, overall	143 mm
Width, overall	30·5 mm
Sights	fixed
Safety	lever
Metal finish	Parkerized
Grip surface	plastic
Breech/system	locked
Inscription	MAC MODELE 1950 CAL. 9 mm

FINLAND

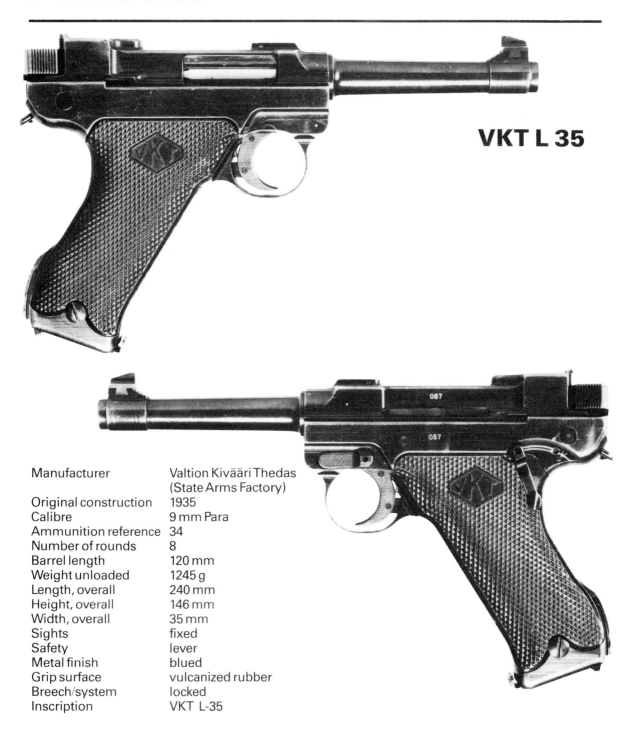

VKT L 35

Manufacturer	Valtion Kivääri Thedas (State Arms Factory)
Original construction	1935
Calibre	9 mm Para
Ammunition reference	34
Number of rounds	8
Barrel length	120 mm
Weight unloaded	1245 g
Length, overall	240 mm
Height, overall	146 mm
Width, overall	35 mm
Sights	fixed
Safety	lever
Metal finish	blued
Grip surface	vulcanized rubber
Breech/system	locked
Inscription	VKT L-35

FINLAND

VKT L 35

Manufacturer	Valtion Metalitehtaat (State Hardware Factory)
Original construction	1935
Calibre	9 mm Para
Ammunition reference	34
Number of rounds	8
Barrel length	117·5 mm
Weight unloaded	1245 g
Length, overall	234·5 mm
Height, overall	146 mm
Width, overall	35 mm
Sights	fixed
Safety	lever
Metal finish	blued
Grip surface	vulcanized rubber
Breech/system	locked
Inscription	VALMET L-35

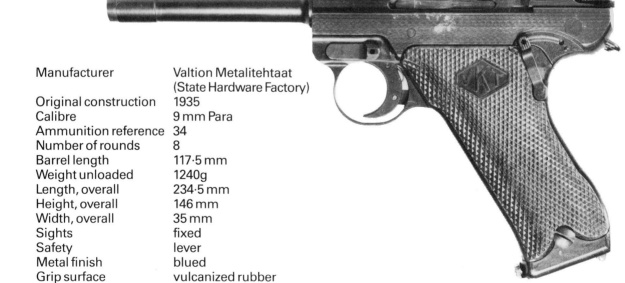

Manufacturer	Valtion Metalitehtaat (State Hardware Factory)
Original construction	1935
Calibre	9 mm Para
Ammunition reference	34
Number of rounds	8
Barrel length	117·5 mm
Weight unloaded	1240g
Length, overall	234·5 mm
Height, overall	146 mm
Width, overall	35 mm
Sights	fixed
Safety	lever
Metal finish	blued
Grip surface	vulcanized rubber
Breech/system	locked
Inscription	VALMET L-35

Manufacturer	Valtion Kivääri Thedas (State Arms Factory)
Original construction	1942
Calibre	9 mm Para
Ammunition reference	34
Number of rounds	8
Barrel length	110 mm
Weight unloaded	1085 g
Length, overall	214 mm
Height, overall	142 mm
Width, overall	36 mm
Sights	fixed
Safety	none
Metal finish	blued
Grip surface	wood
Breech/system	blowback
Inscription	9,00 pist/44 VKT

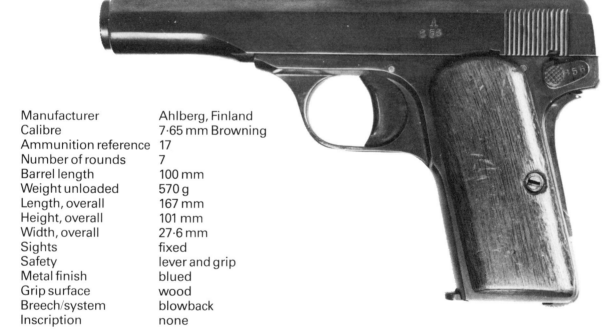

Manufacturer	Ahlberg, Finland
Calibre	7·65 mm Browning
Ammunition reference	17
Number of rounds	7
Barrel length	100 mm
Weight unloaded	570 g
Length, overall	167 mm
Height, overall	101 mm
Width, overall	27·6 mm
Sights	fixed
Safety	lever and grip
Metal finish	blued
Grip surface	wood
Breech/system	blowback
Inscription	none

GERMANY

Adler

Manufacturer	Adlerwerke Engelbrecht u. Wolff, Zella St Blasii
Original construction	1905
Calibre	7·25 mm Adler
Ammunition reference	6
Number of rounds	8
Barrel length	88·5 mm
Weight unloaded	740 g
Length, overall	197 mm
Height, overall	126 mm
Width, overall	30·6 mm
Sights	fixed
Safety	lever
Metal finish	blued
Grip surface	vulcanized rubber
Breech/system	blowback
Inscription	PATENT HAEUSLER ADLERWAFFENWERKE ENGELBRECHT U. WOLFF

GERMANY

Beholla

Manufacturer	Becker u. Holländer, Suhl
Original construction	1915
Calibre	7·65 mm Browning
Ammunition reference	17
Number of rounds	7
Barrel length	74·7 mm
Weight unloaded	620 g
Length, overall	142 mm
Height, overall	103 mm
Width, overall	30 mm
Sights	fixed
Safety	lever
Metal finish	blued
Grip surface	wood
Breech/system	blowback
Inscription	none

Manufacturer	Theodor Bergmann, Gaggenau/Suhl
Original construction	1894
Calibre	8 mm Bergmann
Ammunition reference	23
Number of rounds	5
Barrel length	112·6 mm
Weight unloaded	890 g
Length, overall	255 mm
Height, overall	139 mm
Width, overall	31·9 mm
Sights	fixed
Safety	lever
Metal finish	blued
Grip surface	wood
Breech/system	locked
Inscription	PATENT BREVETE S.G.D.M.

GERMANY

Bergmann 1896 No. 3

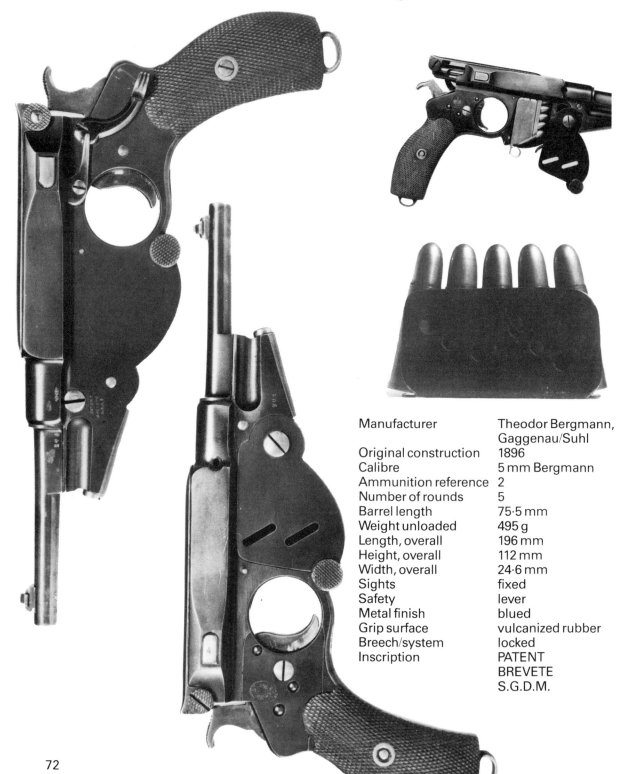

Manufacturer	Theodor Bergmann, Gaggenau/Suhl
Original construction	1896
Calibre	5 mm Bergmann
Ammunition reference	2
Number of rounds	5
Barrel length	75·5 mm
Weight unloaded	495 g
Length, overall	196 mm
Height, overall	112 mm
Width, overall	24·6 mm
Sights	fixed
Safety	lever
Metal finish	blued
Grip surface	vulcanized rubber
Breech/system	locked
Inscription	PATENT BREVETE S.G.D.M.

Manufacturer	Theodor Bergmann, Gaggenau/Suhl
Original construction	1896
Calibre	6·5 mm Bergmann
Ammunition reference	4
Number of rounds	5
Barrel length	112·3 mm
Weight unloaded	880 g
Length, overall	254 mm
Height, overall	141 mm
Width, overall	31·7 mm
Sights	fixed
Safety	lever
Metal finish	blued
Grip surface	wood
Breech/system	locked
Inscription	PATENT BREVETE S.G.D.M.

Manufacturer	Theodor Bergmann, Gaggenau/Suhl
Original construction	1896
Calibre	9 mm Bergmann
Ammunition reference	33
Number of rounds	5
Barrel length	100 mm
Weight unloaded	1155 g
Length, overall	270 mm
Height, overall	146 mm
Width, overall	36·5 mm
Sights	100-1000 m
Safety	lever
Metal finish	blued
Grip surface	vulcanized rubber
Breech/system	locked
Inscription	PISTOLET BERGMANN PATENT BREVETE S.D.G.M.

GERMANY

Bittner Repetier Pistole

(repeater pistol)

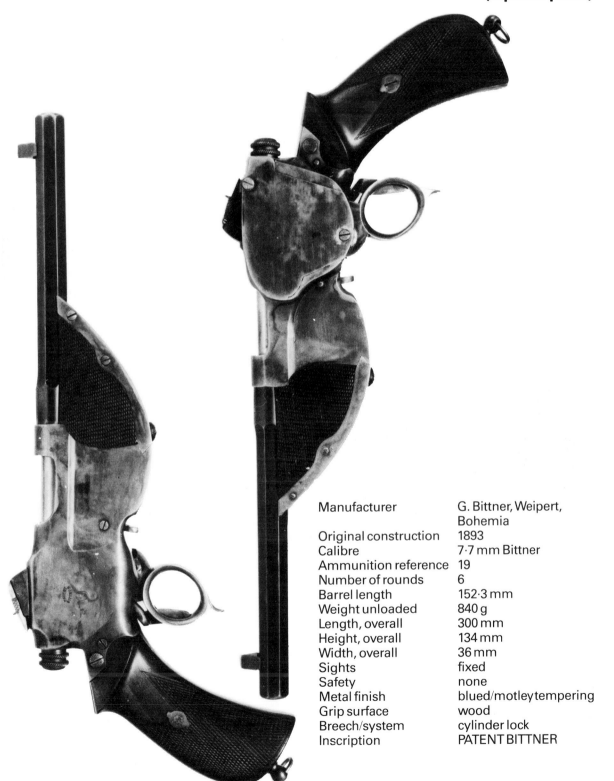

Manufacturer	G. Bittner, Weipert, Bohemia
Original construction	1893
Calibre	7·7 mm Bittner
Ammunition reference	19
Number of rounds	6
Barrel length	152·3 mm
Weight unloaded	840 g
Length, overall	300 mm
Height, overall	134 mm
Width, overall	36 mm
Sights	fixed
Safety	none
Metal finish	blued/motley tempering
Grip surface	wood
Breech/system	cylinder lock
Inscription	PATENT BITTNER

GERMANY

Borchardt

Manufacturer	Waffenfabrik Ludwig Loewe, Berlin
Original construction	1893
Calibre	7·65 mm Borchardt
Ammunition reference	13
Number of rounds	8
Barrel length	190·5 mm
Weight unloaded	1210 g
Length, overall	344·5 mm
Height, overall	138 mm
Width, overall	47 mm
Sights	100-700 m
Safety	slide catch
Metal finish	blued
Grip surface	wood
Breech/system	locked
Inscription	WAFFENFABRIK LOEWE BERLIN D.R.P. No. 75837 SYSTEM BORCHARDT PATENT

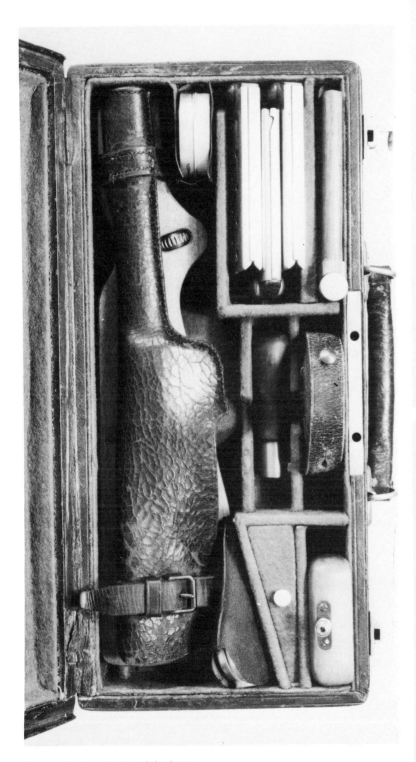

Borchardt shown in its original case

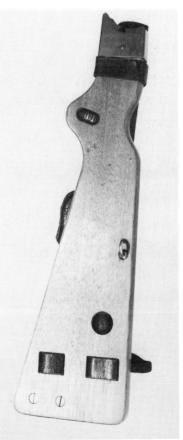

GERMANY

German Ordnance M 79

Manufacturer	F.v. Dreyse, Sömmerda
Original construction	1878
Calibre	10·6 mm German Ordnance
Ammunition reference	47
Number of rounds	6
Barrel length	183·2 mm
Weight unloaded	1330 g
Length, overall	337·5 mm
Height, overall	167 mm
Width, overall	48·4 mm
Sights	fixed
Safety	lever
Metal finish	browned
Grip surface	wood
Breech/system	single action
Inscription	F.V. DREYSE SÖMMERDA

GERMANY

German Ordnance M 79

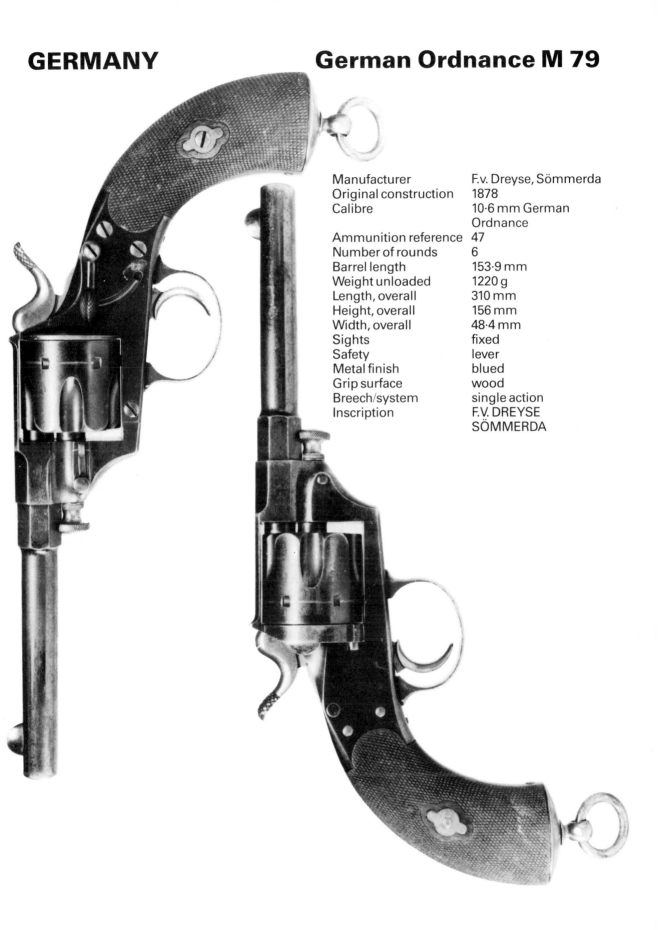

Manufacturer	F.v. Dreyse, Sömmerda
Original construction	1878
Calibre	10·6 mm German Ordnance
Ammunition reference	47
Number of rounds	6
Barrel length	153·9 mm
Weight unloaded	1220 g
Length, overall	310 mm
Height, overall	156 mm
Width, overall	48·4 mm
Sights	fixed
Safety	lever
Metal finish	blued
Grip surface	wood
Breech/system	single action
Inscription	F.V. DREYSE SÖMMERDA

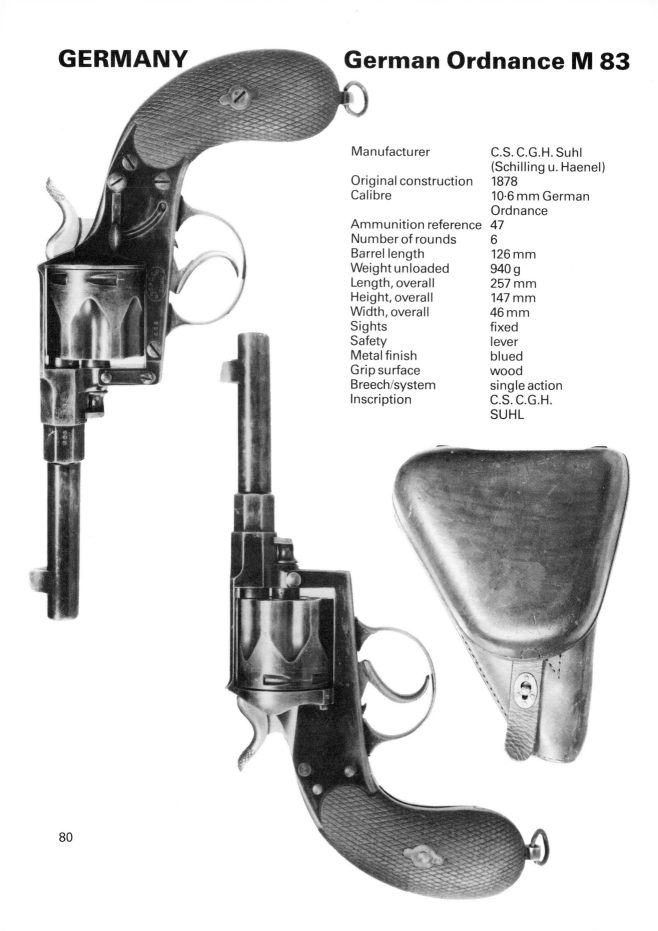

GERMANY

German Ordnance M 83

Manufacturer	C.S. C.G.H. Suhl (Schilling u. Haenel)
Original construction	1878
Calibre	10·6 mm German Ordnance
Ammunition reference	47
Number of rounds	6
Barrel length	126 mm
Weight unloaded	940 g
Length, overall	257 mm
Height, overall	147 mm
Width, overall	46 mm
Sights	fixed
Safety	lever
Metal finish	blued
Grip surface	wood
Breech/system	single action
Inscription	C.S. C.G.H. SUHL

Manufacturer	F.v. Dreyse, Sömmerda
Original construction	1878
Calibre	10·6 mm German Ordnance
Ammunition reference	47
Number of rounds	6
Barrel length	126 mm
Weight unloaded	970 g
Length, overall	258 mm
Height, overall	151 mm
Width, overall	48·5 mm
Sights	fixed
Safety	lever
Metal finish	blued
Grip surface	wood
Breech/system	double action
Inscription	F.V. DREYSE SÖMMERDA

German Ordnance M 83

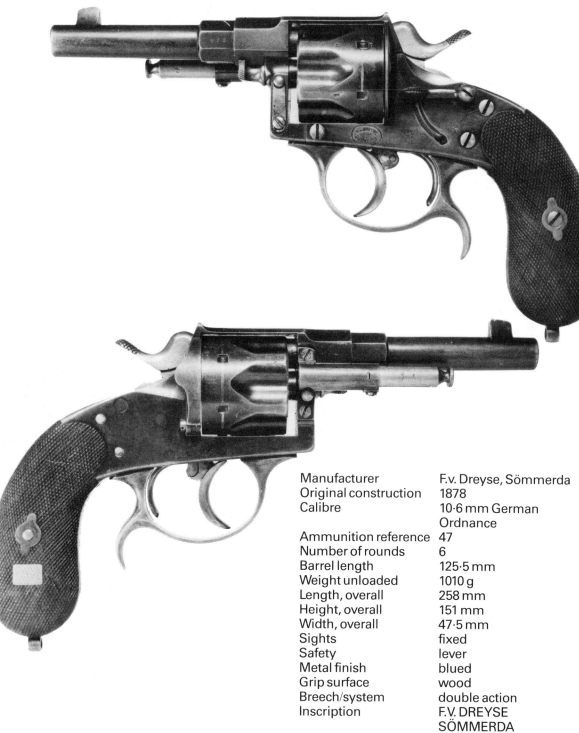

Manufacturer	F.v. Dreyse, Sömmerda
Original construction	1878
Calibre	10·6 mm German Ordnance
Ammunition reference	47
Number of rounds	6
Barrel length	125·5 mm
Weight unloaded	1010 g
Length, overall	258 mm
Height, overall	151 mm
Width, overall	47·5 mm
Sights	fixed
Safety	lever
Metal finish	blued
Grip surface	wood
Breech/system	double action
Inscription	F.V. DREYSE SÖMMERDA

Manufacturer	Rheinische Metallwaaren u. Masch.-Fabrik, Abt. Sömmerda
Original construction	1908
Calibre	7·65 mm Browning
Ammunition reference	17
Number of rounds	7
Barrel length	93 mm
Weight unloaded	660 g
Length, overall	161 mm
Height, overall	119 mm
Width, overall	24·5 mm
Sights	fixed
Safety	lever
Metal finish	blued
Grip surface	vulcanized rubber
Breech/system	blowback
Inscription	DREYSE Rheinische Metall-waaren-§Maschinenfabrik ABT. SÖMMERDA

Dreyse Mod. 07

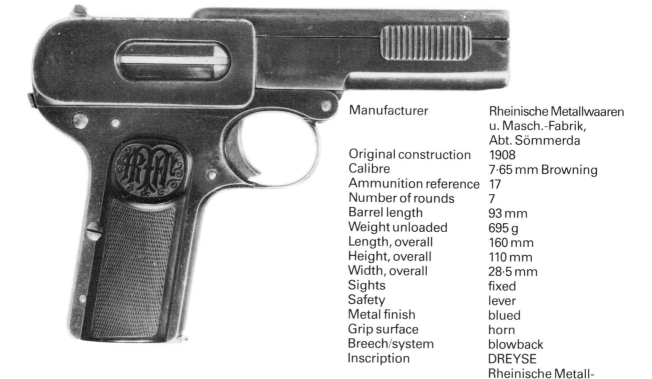

Manufacturer	Rheinische Metallwaaren u. Masch.-Fabrik, Abt. Sömmerda
Original construction	1908
Calibre	7·65 mm Browning
Ammunition reference	17
Number of rounds	7
Barrel length	93 mm
Weight unloaded	695 g
Length, overall	160 mm
Height, overall	110 mm
Width, overall	28·5 mm
Sights	fixed
Safety	lever
Metal finish	blued
Grip surface	horn
Breech/system	blowback
Inscription	DREYSE Rheinische Metall-waaren-§Maschinenfabrik ABT. SÖMMERDA

GERMANY

Dreyse 9 mm Para

Manufacturer	Rheinische Metallwaaren u. Masch.-Fabrik, Abt. Sömmerda
Original construction	1911
Calibre	9 mm Para
Ammunition reference	34
Number of rounds	8
Barrel length	130 mm
Weight unloaded	1120 g
Length, overall	211 mm
Height, overall	136 mm
Width, overall	30·5 mm
Sights	fixed
Safety	lever
Metal finish	blued
Grip surface	horn
Breech/system	blowback
Inscription	DREYSE Rheinische Metall-waaren-§Maschinenfabrik ABT. SÖMMERDA

GERMANY

Langenhan FL Selbstlader

(selfloader)

Manufacturer	Fritz Langenhan
Original construction	1915
Calibre	7·65 mm Browning
Ammunition reference	17
Number of rounds	8
Barrel length	105 mm
Weight unloaded	635 g
Length, overall	168 mm
Height, overall	119 mm
Width, overall	27·4 mm
Sights	fixed
Safety	lever
Metal finish	blued
Grip surface	vulcanized rubber
Breech/system	blowback
Inscription	D.R.P. ANGEM.
	FL SELBSTLADER
	CAL. 7, 65

Langenhan FL Selbstlader

(selfloader)

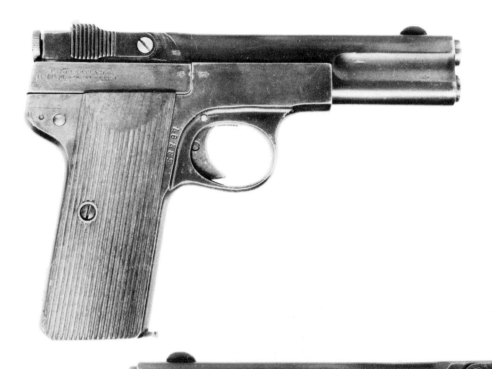

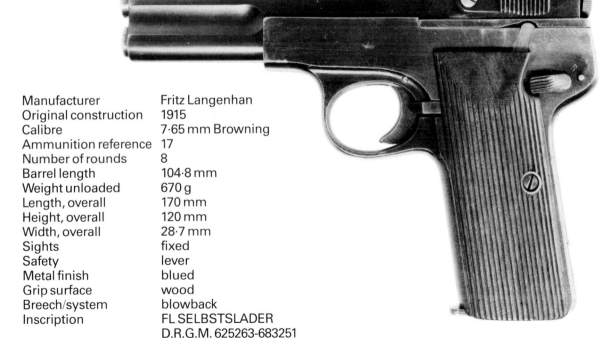

Manufacturer	Fritz Langenhan
Original construction	1915
Calibre	7·65 mm Browning
Ammunition reference	17
Number of rounds	8
Barrel length	104·8 mm
Weight unloaded	670 g
Length, overall	170 mm
Height, overall	120 mm
Width, overall	28·7 mm
Sights	fixed
Safety	lever
Metal finish	blued
Grip surface	wood
Breech/system	blowback
Inscription	FL SELBSTSLADER
	D.R.G.M. 625263-683251

GERMANY   Leonhardt

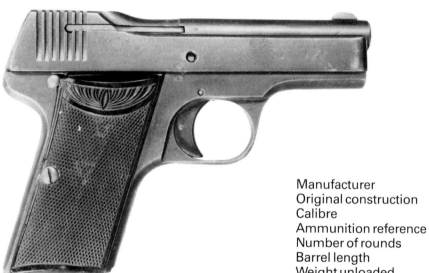

Manufacturer	Menz, Suhl
Original construction	1915
Calibre	7·65 mm Browning
Ammunition reference	17
Number of rounds	7
Barrel length	74·2 mm
Weight unloaded	600 g
Length, overall	142 mm
Height, overall	103 mm
Width, overall	35·7 mm
Sights	fixed
Safety	lever
Metal finish	blued
Grip surface	vulcanized rubber
Breech/system	blowback
Inscription	Selbstlade-Pistole "LEONHARDT"

GERMANY — Mauser C 96 Cone Hammer

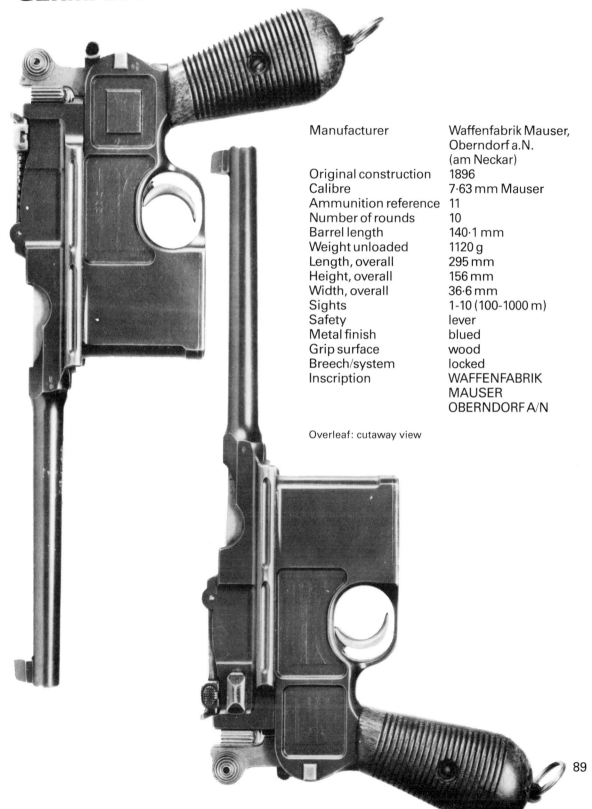

Manufacturer	Waffenfabrik Mauser, Oberndorf a.N. (am Neckar)
Original construction	1896
Calibre	7·63 mm Mauser
Ammunition reference	11
Number of rounds	10
Barrel length	140·1 mm
Weight unloaded	1120 g
Length, overall	295 mm
Height, overall	156 mm
Width, overall	36·6 mm
Sights	1-10 (100-1000 m)
Safety	lever
Metal finish	blued
Grip surface	wood
Breech/system	locked
Inscription	WAFFENFABRIK MAUSER OBERNDORF A/N

Overleaf: cutaway view

Mauser C 96 Cone Hammer

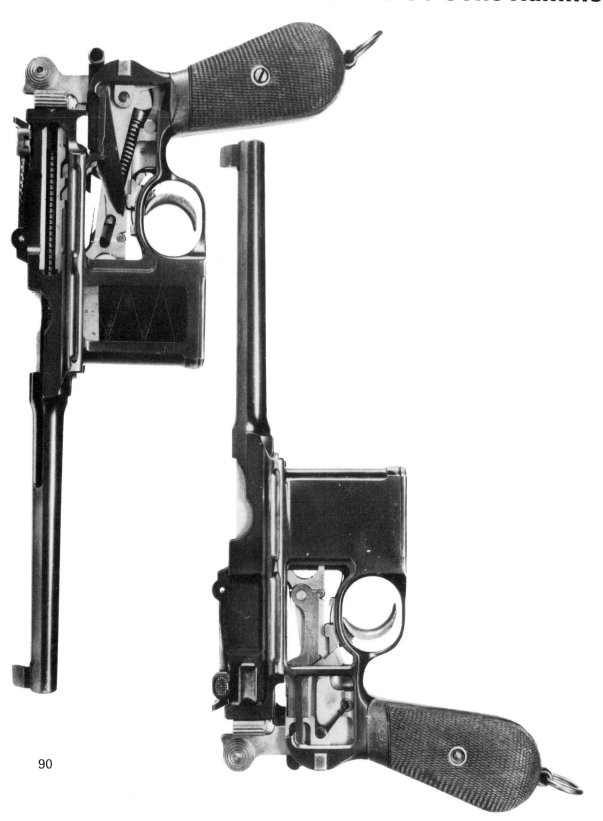

GERMANY   Mauser C 96 Large Ring Mod. 1898

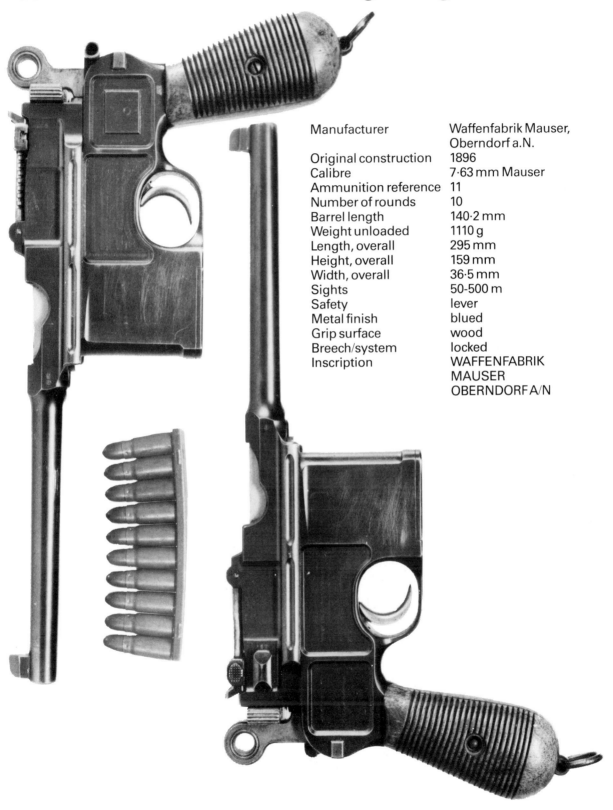

Manufacturer	Waffenfabrik Mauser, Oberndorf a.N.
Original construction	1896
Calibre	7·63 mm Mauser
Ammunition reference	11
Number of rounds	10
Barrel length	140·2 mm
Weight unloaded	1110 g
Length, overall	295 mm
Height, overall	159 mm
Width, overall	36·5 mm
Sights	50-500 m
Safety	lever
Metal finish	blued
Grip surface	wood
Breech/system	locked
Inscription	WAFFENFABRIK MAUSER OBERNDORF A/N

Mauser C 96 Mod. 1905

Manufacturer	Waffenfabrik Mauser, Oberndorf a.N.
Original construction	1896
Calibre	7·63 mm Mauser
Ammunition reference	11
Number of rounds	6
Barrel length	100·8 mm
Weight unloaded	1020 g
Length, overall	254 mm
Height, overall	144 mm
Width, overall	31 mm
Sights	50-1000 m
Safety	lever
Metal finish	blued
Grip surface	wood
Breech/system	locked
Inscription	WAFFENFABRIK MAUSER OBERNDORF A. NECKAR

GERMANY

Mauser C 96 Mod. 1912

Manufacturer	Waffenfabrik Mauser, Oberndorf a.N.
Original construction	1896
Calibre	7·63 mm Mauser
Ammunition reference	11
Number of rounds	10
Barrel length	99·9 mm
Weight unloaded	1040 g
Length, overall	251 mm
Height, overall	146 mm
Width, overall	30·9 mm
Sights	50-1000 m
Safety	lever
Metal finish	blued
Grip surface	wood
Breech/system	locked
Inscription	WAFFENFABRIK MAUSER OBERNDORF A.N.

Overleaf: wooden holster and shoulder stock

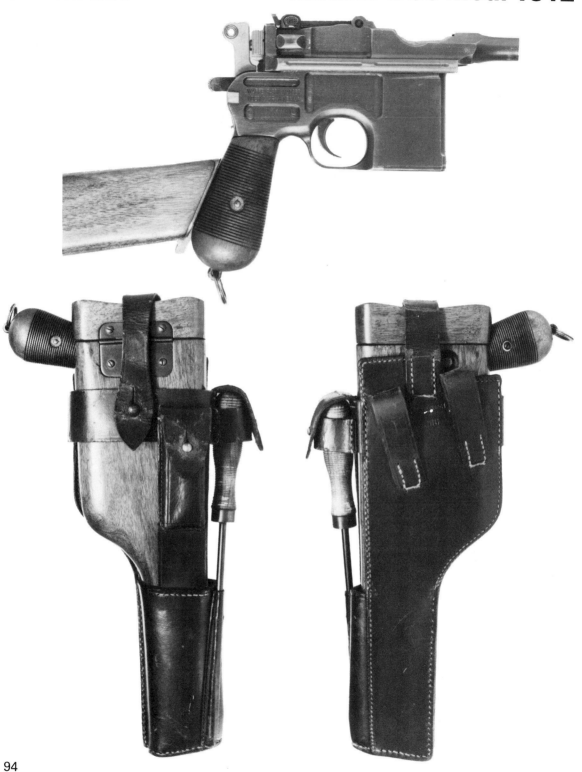

GERMANY

Mauser C 96 Mod. 1916

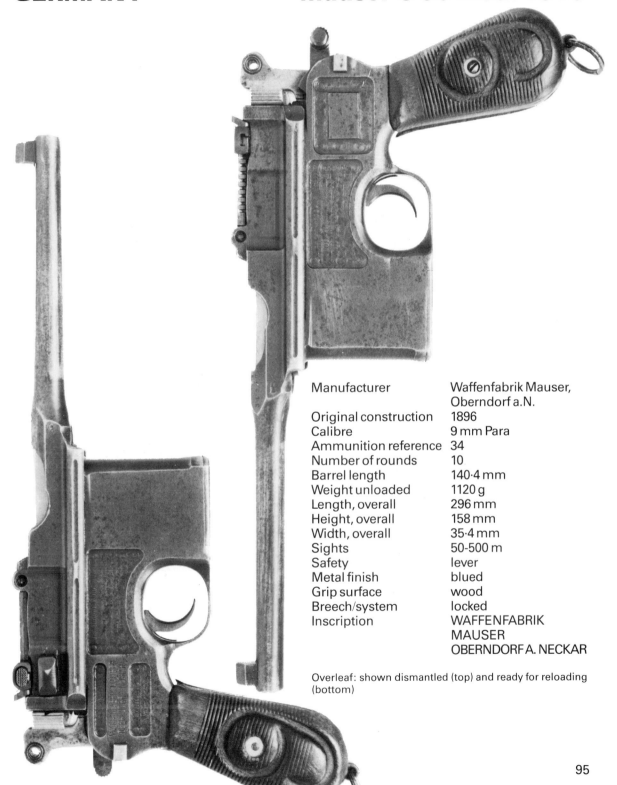

Manufacturer	Waffenfabrik Mauser, Oberndorf a.N.
Original construction	1896
Calibre	9 mm Para
Ammunition reference	34
Number of rounds	10
Barrel length	140·4 mm
Weight unloaded	1120 g
Length, overall	296 mm
Height, overall	158 mm
Width, overall	35·4 mm
Sights	50-500 m
Safety	lever
Metal finish	blued
Grip surface	wood
Breech/system	locked
Inscription	WAFFENFABRIK MAUSER OBERNDORF A. NECKAR

Overleaf: shown dismantled (top) and ready for reloading (bottom)

95

Mauser C 96 Mod. 1916

Mauser C 96 Mod. 1920

Manufacturer	Waffenfabrik Mauser, Oberndorf a.N.
Original construction	1896
Calibre	7·63 mm Mauser
Ammunition reference	11
Number of rounds	10
Barrel length	99·6 mm

Weight unloaded	1045 g
Length, overall	251 mm
Height, overall	146 mm
Width, overall	30·9 mm
Sights	50-1000 m
Safety	lever
Metal finish	blued
Grip surface	wood
Breech/system	locked
Inscription	WAFFENFABRIK MAUSER OBERNDORF A. NECKAR

Mauser C 96 Mod. 1930

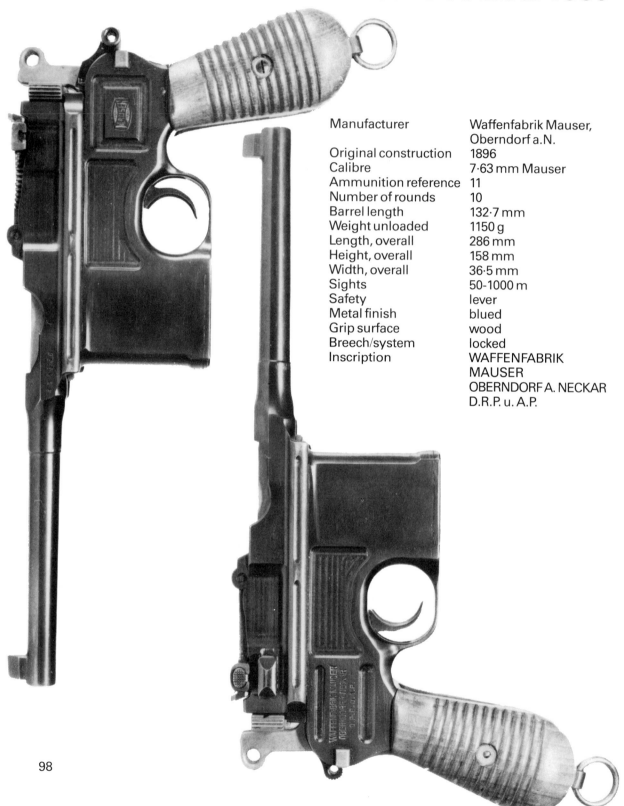

Manufacturer	Waffenfabrik Mauser, Oberndorf a.N.
Original construction	1896
Calibre	7·63 mm Mauser
Ammunition reference	11
Number of rounds	10
Barrel length	132·7 mm
Weight unloaded	1150 g
Length, overall	286 mm
Height, overall	158 mm
Width, overall	36·5 mm
Sights	50-1000 m
Safety	lever
Metal finish	blued
Grip surface	wood
Breech/system	locked
Inscription	WAFFENFABRIK MAUSER OBERNDORF A. NECKAR D.R.P. u. A.P.

GERMANY

Mauser Mod. 1932

Manufacturer	Waffenfabrik Mauser, Oberndorf a.N.
Original construction	1896
Calibre	7·63 mm Mauser
Ammunition reference	11
Number of rounds	10 or 20
Barrel length	132·8 mm
Weight unloaded	1285 g
Length, overall	288 mm
Height, overall	155 mm
Width, overall	30 mm
Sights	50-1000 m
Safety	lever
Metal finish	blued
Grip surface	wood
Breech/system	locked
Inscription	WAFFENFABRIK MAUSER OBERNDORF A. NECKAR D.R.P. u. A.P.

Manufacturer	Waffenfabrik Mauser AG, Oberndorf a.N.
Original construction	unknown
Calibre	9 mm Nickl
Ammunition reference	–
Number of rounds	7
Barrel length	87 mm
Weight unloaded	580 g
Length, overall	149 mm
Height, overall	124 mm
Width, overall	29 mm
Sights	fixed
Safety	lever
Metal finish	blued
Grip surface	wood
Breech/system	blow-back
Inscription	Waffenfabrik Mauser AG Oberndorf a.N.

Manufacturer	Waffenfabrik Mauser, Oberndorf a. N.
Original construction	1912/14
Calibre	9 mm Mauser Versuch III (Experimental III)
Ammunition reference	38
Number of rounds	8
Barrel length	99 mm
Weight unloaded	970 g
Length, overall	182 mm
Height, overall	140 mm
Width, overall	32 mm
Sights	fixed
Safety	lever
Metal finish	blued
Grip surface	wood
Breech/system	locked
Inscription	WAFFENFABRIK MAUSER OBERNDORF A.N. MAUSER'S PATENT

GERMANY

Mauser Mod. 1914

Manufacturer	Mauser-Werke, Oberndorf a. N.
Original construction	1914
Calibre	7·65 mm Browning
Ammunition reference	17
Number of rounds	8
Barrel length	87 mm
Weight unloaded	610 g
Length, overall	154 mm
Height, overall	115 mm
Width, overall	26·5 mm
Sights	fixed
Safety	lever
Metal finish	blued
Grip surface	wood
Breech/system	blowback
Inscription	MAUSER-WERKE A. G. OBERNDORF A. N. CAL. 7, 65

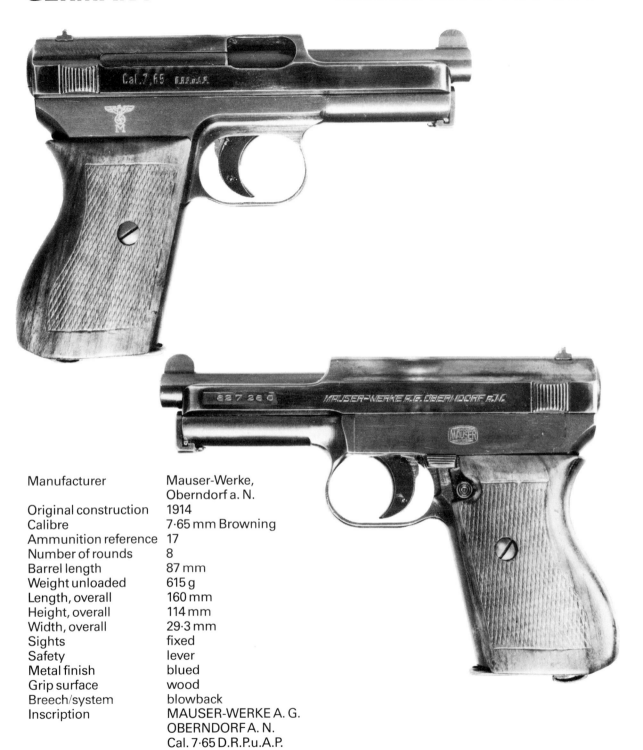

Manufacturer	Mauser-Werke, Oberndorf a. N.
Original construction	1914
Calibre	7·65 mm Browning
Ammunition reference	17
Number of rounds	8
Barrel length	87 mm
Weight unloaded	615 g
Length, overall	160 mm
Height, overall	114 mm
Width, overall	29·3 mm
Sights	fixed
Safety	lever
Metal finish	blued
Grip surface	wood
Breech/system	blowback
Inscription	MAUSER-WERKE A. G. OBERNDORF A. N. Cal. 7·65 D.R.P.u.A.P.

Manufacturer	Mauser-Werke, Oberndorf a. N.
Original construction	1937
Calibre	7·65 mm Browning
Ammunition reference	17
Number of rounds	8
Barrel length	86 mm
Weight unloaded	645 g
Length, overall	163 mm
Height, overall	111 mm
Width, overall	28·3 mm
Sights	fixed
Safety	lever
Metal finish	blued
Grip surface	wood
Breech/system	blowback
Inscription	Mauser-Werke A.G. Oberndorf a. N. Mod. HSc Kal. 7,65 mm

GERMANY

Menta

Manufacturer	August Menz, Suhl
Original construction	1915
Calibre	7·65 mm Browning
Ammunition reference	17
Number of rounds	7
Barrel length	73 mm
Weight unloaded	620 g
Length, overall	142 mm
Height, overall	101 mm
Width, overall	25·2 mm
Sights	fixed
Safety	lever
Metal finish	blued
Grip surface	vulcanized rubber
Breech/system	blowback
Inscription	"MENTA" KAL. 7,65

Manufacturer	Deutsche Werke A.G., Erfurt
Calibre	7·65 mm Browning
Ammunition reference	17
Number of rounds	8
Barrel length	87 mm
Weight unloaded	630 g
Length, overall	164 mm
Height, overall	111 mm
Width, overall	30·2 mm
Sights	fixed
Safety	press-button and grip lever
Metal finish	blued
Grip surface	wood
Breech/system	blowback
Inscription	DEUTSCHE WERKE WERK ERFURT ORTGIES' PATENT

GERMANY

Ortgies

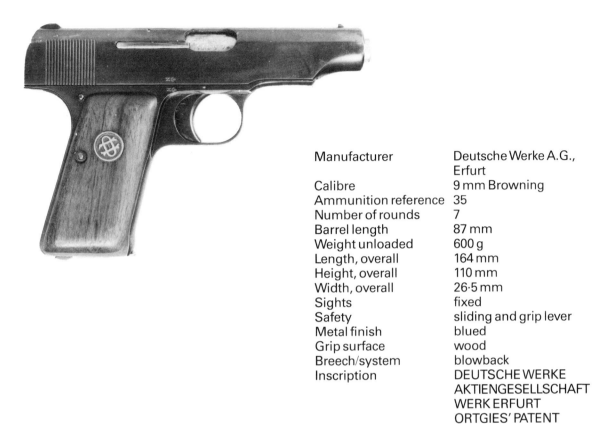

Manufacturer	Deutsche Werke A.G., Erfurt
Calibre	9 mm Browning
Ammunition reference	35
Number of rounds	7
Barrel length	87 mm
Weight unloaded	600 g
Length, overall	164 mm
Height, overall	110 mm
Width, overall	26·5 mm
Sights	fixed
Safety	sliding and grip lever
Metal finish	blued
Grip surface	wood
Breech/system	blowback
Inscription	DEUTSCHE WERKE AKTIENGESELLSCHAFT WERK ERFURT ORTGIES' PATENT

Pistole 08 Mod. 1904

Manufacturer	Deutsche Waffen- und Munitionsfabrik
Original construction	1900
Calibre	9 mm Para
Ammunition reference	34
Number of rounds	8
Barrel length	152 mm
Weight unloaded	970 g
Length, overall	269 mm
Height, overall	144 mm
Width, overall	38·7 mm
Sights	100 and 200 m
Safety	lever and grip
Metal finish	blued
Grip surface	wood
Breech/system	locked
Inscription	DWM

GERMANY

Pistole 08 Mod. 1917
(Lange Pistole 08)

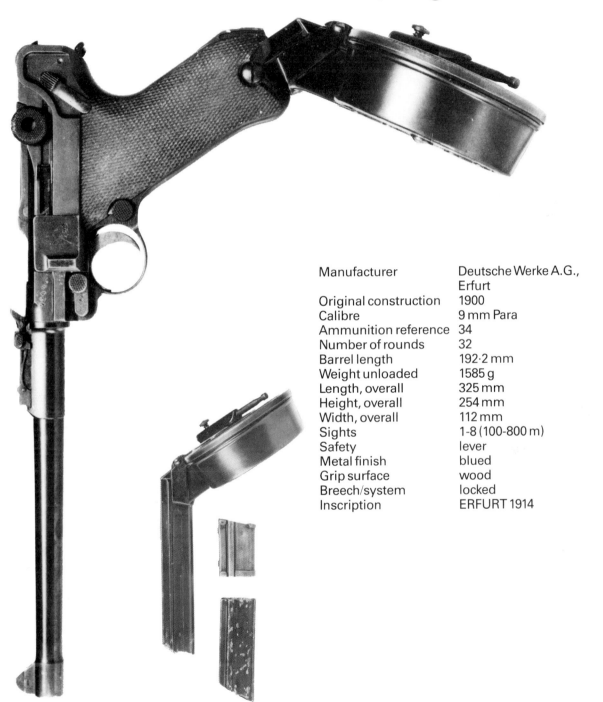

Manufacturer	Deutsche Werke A.G., Erfurt
Original construction	1900
Calibre	9 mm Para
Ammunition reference	34
Number of rounds	32
Barrel length	192·2 mm
Weight unloaded	1585 g
Length, overall	325 mm
Height, overall	254 mm
Width, overall	112 mm
Sights	1-8 (100-800 m)
Safety	lever
Metal finish	blued
Grip surface	wood
Breech/system	locked
Inscription	ERFURT 1914

GERMANY

Pistole 08 Mod. 1917
(Lange Pistole 08)

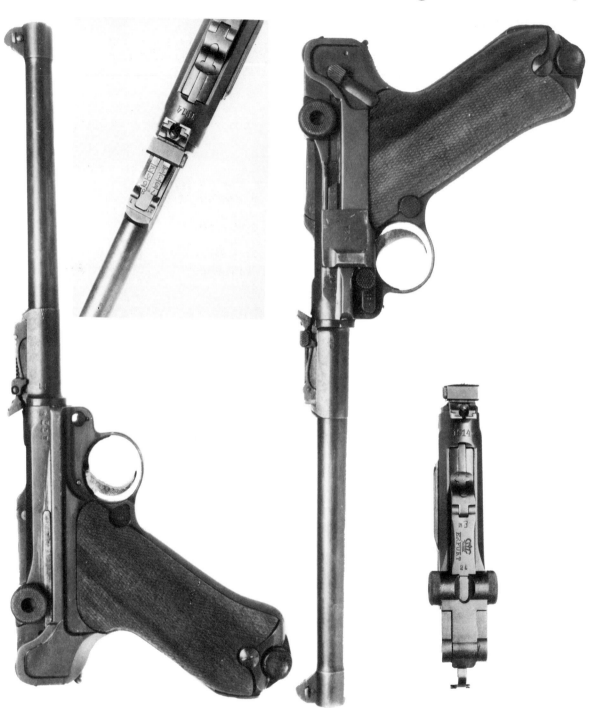

GERMANY

Pistole 08 (Finland)

Manufacturer	Deutsche Waffen- und Munitionsfabrik
Original construction	1900
Calibre	7·65 mm Para
Ammunition reference	15
Number of rounds	8
Barrel length	96 mm
Weight unloaded	890 g
Length, overall	215 mm
Height, overall	138 mm
Width, overall	38·6 mm
Sights	fixed
Safety	lever
Metal finish	blued
Grip surface	wood
Breech/system	locked
Inscription	DWM

GERMANY   Pistole 08 Mod. 1934 (Persia/Iran)

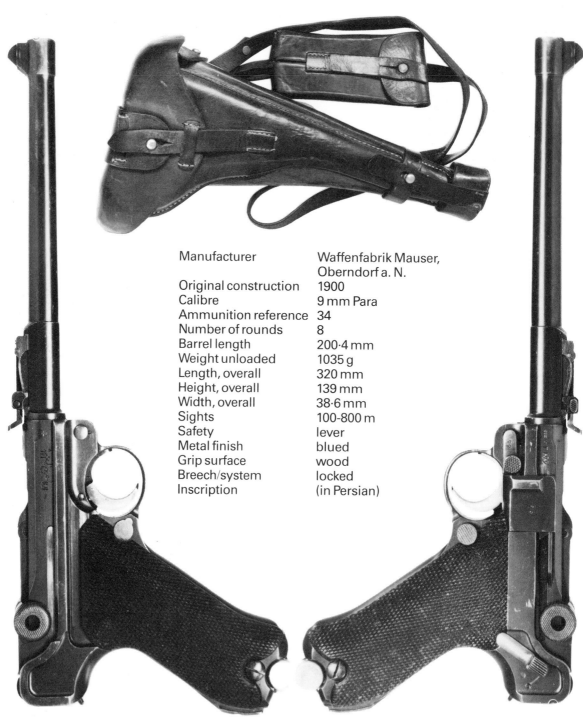

Manufacturer	Waffenfabrik Mauser, Oberndorf a. N.
Original construction	1900
Calibre	9 mm Para
Ammunition reference	34
Number of rounds	8
Barrel length	200·4 mm
Weight unloaded	1035 g
Length, overall	320 mm
Height, overall	139 mm
Width, overall	38·6 mm
Sights	100-800 m
Safety	lever
Metal finish	blued
Grip surface	wood
Breech/system	locked
Inscription	(in Persian)

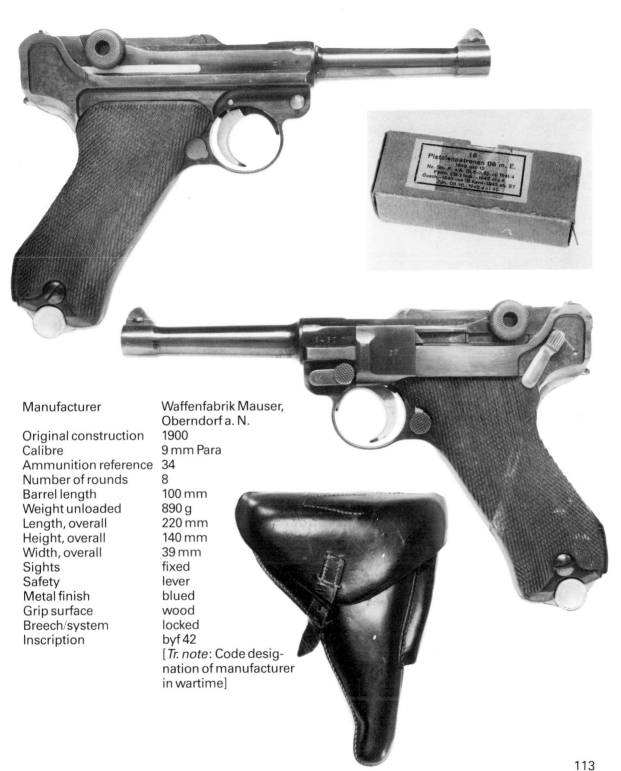

Manufacturer	Waffenfabrik Mauser, Oberndorf a. N.
Original construction	1900
Calibre	9 mm Para
Ammunition reference	34
Number of rounds	8
Barrel length	100 mm
Weight unloaded	890 g
Length, overall	220 mm
Height, overall	140 mm
Width, overall	39 mm
Sights	fixed
Safety	lever
Metal finish	blued
Grip surface	wood
Breech/system	locked
Inscription	byf 42 [*Tr. note*: Code designation of manufacturer in wartime]

Manufacturer	Waffenfabrik Mauser, Oberndorf a. N.
Original construction	1900
Calibre	9 mm Para
Ammunition reference	34
Number of rounds	8
Barrel length	100 mm
Weight unloaded	885 g
Length, overall	220 mm
Height, overall	140 mm
Width, overall	39 mm
Sights	fixed
Safety	lever
Metal finish	blued
Grip surface	bakelite
Breech/system	locked
Inscription	byf 42

GERMANY

Sauer & Sohn Mod. 1913

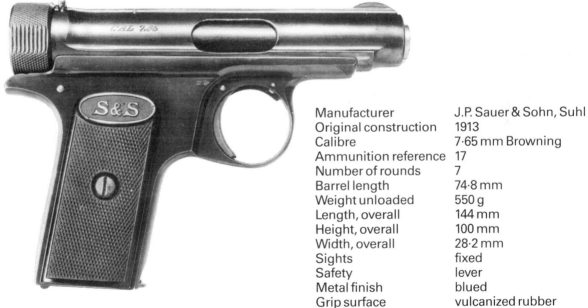

Manufacturer	J.P. Sauer & Sohn, Suhl
Original construction	1913
Calibre	7·65 mm Browning
Ammunition reference	17
Number of rounds	7
Barrel length	74·8 mm
Weight unloaded	550 g
Length, overall	144 mm
Height, overall	100 mm
Width, overall	28·2 mm
Sights	fixed
Safety	lever
Metal finish	blued
Grip surface	vulcanized rubber
Breech/system	blowback
Inscription	J.P. SAUER & SOHN SUHL CAL. 7,65 PATENT

GERMANY   Sauer & Sohn Mod. 1913

Manufacturer	J.P. Sauer & Sohn, Suhl
Original construction	1913
Calibre	7·65 mm Browning
Ammunition reference	17
Number of rounds	7
Barrel length	88·5 mm
Weight unloaded	545 g
Length, overall	145 mm
Height, overall	110 mm
Width, overall	26·7 mm
Sights	fixed
Safety	lever
Metal finish	blued
Grip surface	vulcanized rubber
Breech/system	blowback
Inscription	J.P. SAUER & SOHN
	SUHL
	PATENT CAL. 7,65

GERMANY   Sauer & Sohn Mod. 1930

Manufacturer	J.P. Sauer & Sohn, Suhl
Original construction	1930
Calibre	7·65 mm Browning
Ammunition reference	17
Number of rounds	7
Barrel length	77 mm
Weight unloaded	620 g
Length, overall	148 mm
Height, overall	112 mm
Width, overall	25·8 mm
Sights	fixed
Safety	lever
Metal finish	blued
Grip surface	vulcanized rubber
Breech/system	blowback
Inscription	J.P. SAUER & SOHN
	SUHL
	CAL. 7,65
	PATENT

GERMANY   Sauer & Sohn Mod. 1938

Manufacturer	Sauer & Sohn, Suhl
Original construction	1938
Calibre	7·65 mm Browning
Ammunition reference	17
Number of rounds	8
Barrel length	86·5 mm
Weight unloaded	705 g
Length, overall	160 mm
Height, overall	113 mm
Width, overall	30 mm
Sights	fixed
Safety	lever
Metal finish	blued
Grip surface	vulcanized rubber
Breech/system	blowback
Inscription	J.P. SAUER & SOHN SUHL CAL. 7,65 PATENT

GERMANY

Schlegelmilch

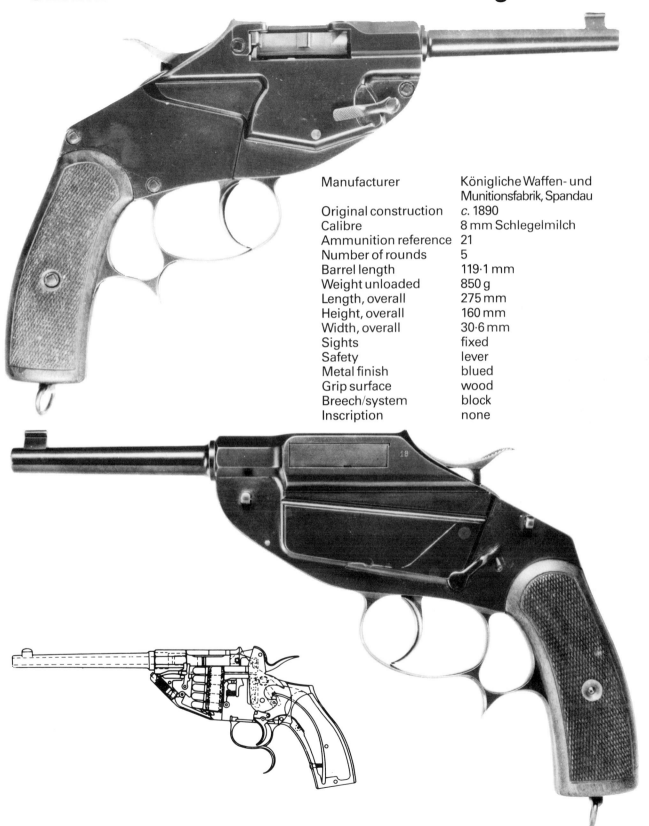

Manufacturer	Königliche Waffen- und Munitionsfabrik, Spandau
Original construction	*c.* 1890
Calibre	8 mm Schlegelmilch
Ammunition reference	21
Number of rounds	5
Barrel length	119·1 mm
Weight unloaded	850 g
Length, overall	275 mm
Height, overall	160 mm
Width, overall	30·6 mm
Sights	fixed
Safety	lever
Metal finish	blued
Grip surface	wood
Breech/system	block
Inscription	none

Manufacturer	Franz Stock, Berlin
Original construction	1925
Calibre	7·65 mm Browning
Ammunition reference	17
Number of rounds	8
Barrel length	100 mm
Weight unloaded	670 g
Length, overall	170 mm
Height, overall	108 mm
Width, overall	29·2 mm
Sights	fixed
Safety	lever
Metal finish	blued
Grip surface	vulcanized rubber
Breech/system	blowback
Inscription	FRANZ STOCK-BERLIN D.R.P. CAL. 7,65

Manufacturer	Carl Walther, Zella St. Blasii
Original construction	1910
Calibre	7·65 mm Browning
Ammunition reference	17
Number of rounds	8
Barrel length	88·1 mm
Weight unloaded	540 g
Length, overall	151 mm
Height, overall	108 mm
Width, overall	28·5 mm
Sights	fixed
Safety	lever
Metal finish	blued
Grip surface	vulcanized rubber
Breech/system	blowback
Inscription	SELBSTLADE-PISTOLE CAL. 7,65 WALTHER'S PATENT Carl Walther. WAFFENFABRIK Zella St. Blasii

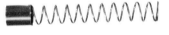

Manufacturer	Carl Walther, Zella-Mehlis
Original construction	1910
Calibre	7·65 mm Browning
Ammunition reference	17
Number of rounds	8
Barrel length	88·2 mm
Weight unloaded	545 g
Length, overall	152 mm
Height, overall	108 mm
Width, overall	26 mm
Sights	fixed
Safety	lever
Metal finish	blued
Grip surface	vulcanized rubber
Breech/system	blowback
Inscription	WALTHER'S-PATENT CAL. 7,65 WAFFENFABRIK WALTHER ZELLA-MEHLIS

Manufacturer	Walther, Zella St. Blasii
Original construction	1910
Calibre	9 mm Para
Ammunition reference	34
Number of rounds	8
Barrel length	123·4 mm
Weight unloaded	890 g
Length, overall	205 mm
Height, overall	136 mm
Width, overall	34 mm
Sights	fixed
Safety	lever
Metal finish	blued
Grip surface	vulcanized rubber
Breech/system	blowback
Inscription	Selbstlade-Pistole Cal. 9 m/m, Walther's-Patent, Carl Walther, Waffenfabrik, Zella St. Bl.

Manufacturer	Walther, Zella-Mehlis
Original construction	1936
Calibre	9 mm Para
Ammunition reference	34
Number of rounds	8
Barrel length	127·3 mm
Weight unloaded	965 g
Length, overall	215 mm
Height, overall	138 mm
Width, overall	36 mm
Sights	fixed
Safety	lever
Metal finish	blued
Grip surface	bakelite
Breech/system	locked
Inscription	Waffenfabrik Walther Zella-Mehlis (Thür.) Mod. HP Walther's Patent Cal. 9 m/m

GERMANY   Walther Mod. HP (Sweden)

Manufacturer	Waffenfabrik Walther, Zella-Mehlis
Original construction	1936
Calibre	9 mm Para
Ammunition reference	34
Number of rounds	8
Barrel length	124·8 mm
Weight unloaded	950 g
Length, overall	214 mm
Height, overall	139 mm
Width, overall	36·4 mm
Sights	fixed
Safety	lever
Metal finish	blued
Grip surface	bakelite
Breech/system	locked
Inscription	Waffenfabrik Walther Zella-Mehlis (Thür.) Walther's Patent Cal. 9 mm Mod. HP

Walther P 38 K

Manufacturer	Waffenfabrik Walther, Zella-Mehlis (Thür.)
Original construction	1936
Calibre	9 mm Para
Ammunition reference	34
Number of rounds	8
Barrel length	101 mm
Weight unloaded	830 g
Length, overall	168 mm
Height, overall	120 mm
Width, overall	33·2 mm
Sights	fixed
Safety	lever
Metal finish	blued
Grip surface	wood
Breech/system	locked
Inscription	Waffenfabrik Walther Zella-Mehlis (Thür.) Walther's Patent Mod. P 38 "K"

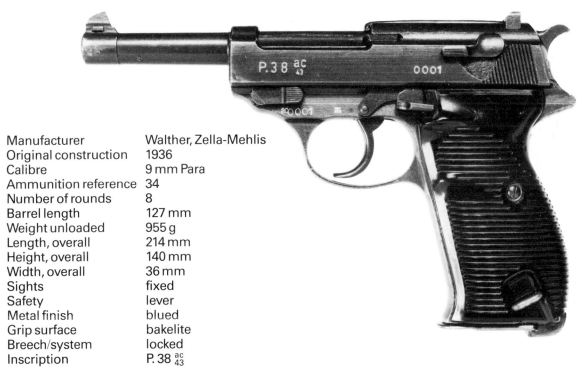

Manufacturer	Walther, Zella-Mehlis
Original construction	1936
Calibre	9 mm Para
Ammunition reference	34
Number of rounds	8
Barrel length	127 mm
Weight unloaded	955 g
Length, overall	214 mm
Height, overall	140 mm
Width, overall	36 mm
Sights	fixed
Safety	lever
Metal finish	blued
Grip surface	bakelite
Breech/system	locked
Inscription	P. 38 $^{ac}_{43}$

GERMANY

Walther P 38

Manufacturer	Waffenfabrik Mauser, Oberndorf a. N.
Original construction	1936
Calibre	9 mm Para
Ammunition reference	34
Number of rounds	8
Barrel length	124·6 mm
Weight unloaded	955 g
Length, overall	214 mm
Height, overall	138 mm
Width, overall	36 mm
Sights	fixed
Safety	lever
Metal finish	blued
Grip surface	bakelite
Breech/system	locked
Inscription	P. 38 $^{byt}_{43}$

Manufacturer	Walther, Zella-Mehlis
Original construction	1936
Calibre	9 mm Para
Ammunition reference	34
Number of rounds	8
Barrel length	127 mm
Weight unloaded	1035 g
Length, overall	214 mm
Height, overall	140 mm
Width, overall	36 mm
Sights	fixed
Safety	lever
Metal finish	Parkerized
Grip surface	sheet metal
Breech/system	locked
Inscription	P. 38 $^{svw}_{45}$

GERMANY

Walther P 38

Manufacturer	Waffenfabrik Walther, Zella-Mehlis
Original construction	1936
Calibre	9 mm Para
Ammunition reference	34
Number of rounds	8
Barrel length	127 mm
Weight unloaded	955 g
Length, overall	216 mm
Height, overall	138 mm
Width, overall	36 mm
Sights	fixed
Safety	lever
Metal finish	phosphated
Grip surface	bakelite
Breech/system	locked
Inscription	none

GERMANY

Walther PP

Manufacturer	Waffenfabrik Walther, Zella-Mehlis
Original construction	1924
Calibre	7·65 mm Browning
Ammunition reference	17
Number of rounds	8
Barrel length	97·9 mm
Weight unloaded	675 g
Length, overall	170 mm
Height, overall	122 mm
Width, overall	30·4 mm
Sights	fixed
Safety	lever
Metal finish	blued
Grip surface	vulcanized rubber
Breech/system	blowback
Inscription	Waffenfabrik Walther. Zella-Mehlis (Thür.) Walther's Patent Cal. 7,65 m/m Mod. PP

131

Manufacturer	Waffenfabrik Walther, Zella-Mehlis
Original construction	1924
Calibre	7·65 mm Browning
Ammunition reference	17
Number of rounds	7
Barrel length	83·6 mm
Weight unloaded	570 g
Length, overall	154 mm
Height, overall	105 mm
Width, overall	25·7 mm
Sights	fixed
Safety	lever
Metal finish	blued
Grip surface	vulcanized rubber
Breech/system	blowback
Inscription	Waffenfabrik Walther, Zella-Mehlis (Thür.) Walther's Patent Cal. 7,65 m/m Mod. PPK

GERMANY

Werder-Pistole Mod. 69

Manufacturer	Waffenfabrik Amberg
Original construction	1869
Calibre	11 mm Werder
Ammunition reference	52
Number of rounds	1
Barrel length	224·5 mm
Weight unloaded	1645 g
Length, overall	377 mm
Height, overall	175 mm
Width, overall	40 mm
Sights	fixed
Safety	lever
Metal finish	blued
Grip surface	wood
Breech/system	falling block
Inscription	none

UK

Enfield Mk II Mod. 1882

Manufacturer	Royal Small Arms Factory, Enfield
Original construction	1880
Calibre	·476 Eley
Ammunition reference	61
Number of rounds	6
Barrel length	148 mm
Weight unloaded	1130 g
Length, overall	293 mm
Height, overall	158 mm
Width, overall	46·2 mm
Sights	fixed
Safety	none
Metal finish	blued
Grip surface	wood
Breech/system	double-action
Inscription	none

Manufacturer	Royal Small Arms Factory, Enfield
Original construction	1927
Calibre	·38/200
Ammunition reference	42/43
Number of rounds	6
Barrel length	127 mm
Weight unloaded	770 g
Length, overall	255 mm
Height, overall	145 mm
Width, overall	37·1 mm
Sights	fixed
Safety	none
Metal finish	blued
Grip surface	wood
Breech/system	double-action
Inscription	ENFIELD No. 2 Mk I 1937

Manufacturer	Royal Small Arms Factory, Enfield
Original construction	1927
Calibre	·38/200
Ammunition reference	42/43
Number of rounds	6
Barrel length	126·6 mm
Weight unloaded	785 g
Length, overall	255 mm
Height, overall	146 mm
Width, overall	37 mm
Sights	fixed
Safety	none
Metal finish	Parkerized
Grip surface	vulcanized rubber
Breech/system	double-action
Inscription	none

Manufacturer	Royal Small Arms Factory, Enfield
Original construction	1927
Calibre	·38/200
Ammunition reference	42/43
Number of rounds	6
Barrel length	76 mm
Weight unloaded	700 g
Length, overall	206 mm
Height, overall	131 mm
Width, overall	37·2 mm
Sights	fixed
Safety	none
Metal finish	Parkerized
Grip surface	wood
Breech/system	double-action
Inscription	ENFIELD No. 2 Mk I 1932

Manufacturer	The Brändlin Armoury Company Ltd., Birmingham
Original construction	*c.* 1869
Calibre	·442 Eley
Ammunition reference	54
Number of rounds	5
Barrel length	145·5 mm
Weight unloaded	960 g
Length, overall	271 mm
Height, overall	132 mm
Width, overall	43·9 mm
Sights	fixed
Safety	none
Metal finish	blued
Grip surface	wood
Breech/system	double-action
Inscription	GALAND SOMMERVILLE

Pistolet Mars

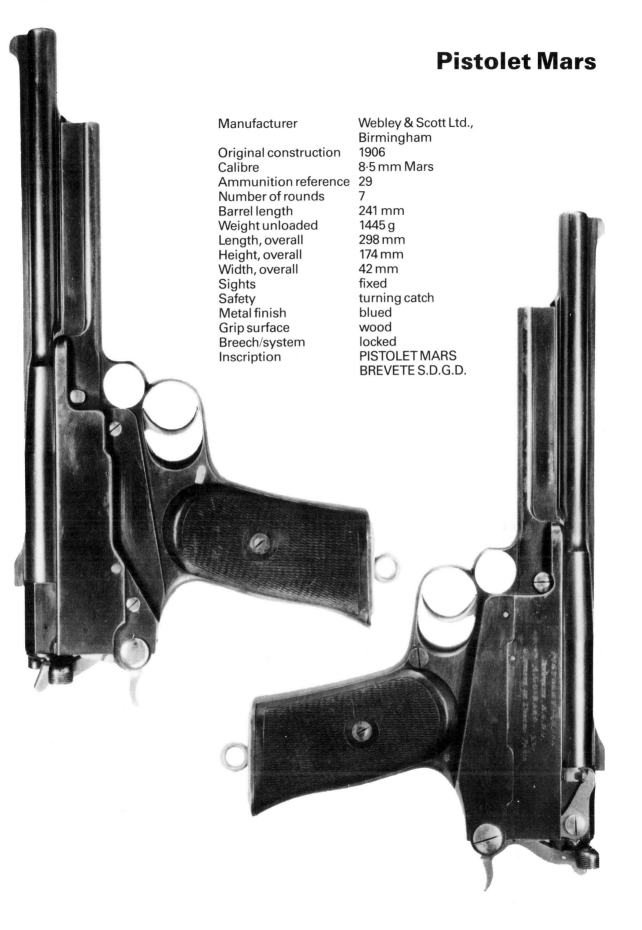

Manufacturer	Webley & Scott Ltd., Birmingham
Original construction	1906
Calibre	8·5 mm Mars
Ammunition reference	29
Number of rounds	7
Barrel length	241 mm
Weight unloaded	1445 g
Length, overall	298 mm
Height, overall	174 mm
Width, overall	42 mm
Sights	fixed
Safety	turning catch
Metal finish	blued
Grip surface	wood
Breech/system	locked
Inscription	PISTOLET MARS BREVETE S.D.G.D.

Manufacturer	Webley & Son, London & Birmingham
Original construction	1899
Calibre	·455 Webley
Ammunition reference	56-59
Number of rounds	6
Barrel length	103 mm
Weight unloaded	960 g
Length, overall	235 mm
Height, overall	148 mm
Width, overall	43·6 mm
Sights	fixed
Safety	none
Metal finish	blued
Grip surface	vulcanized rubber
Breech/system	double-action
Inscription	P. WEBLEY & SON LONDON & BIRMINGHAM MARK IV WEBLEY PATENTS

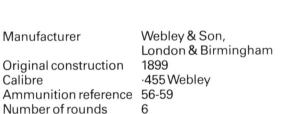

Manufacturer	Webley & Son, London & Birmingham
Original construction	1899
Calibre	·455 Webley
Ammunition reference	56-59
Number of rounds	6
Barrel length	154·2 mm
Weight unloaded	1005 g
Length, overall	284 mm
Height, overall	154 mm
Width, overall	43·6 mm
Sights	fixed
Safety	none
Metal finish	blued
Grip surface	wood
Breech/system	double-action
Inscription	WEBLEY MARK IV PATENTS

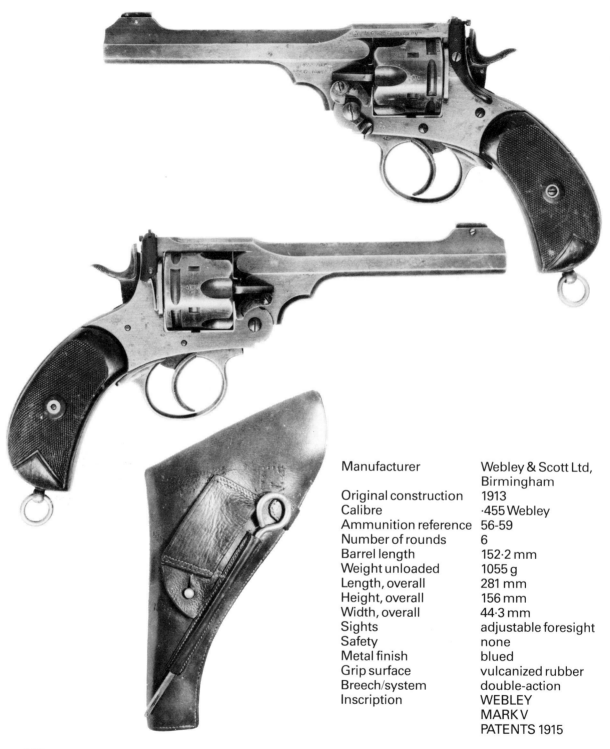

Manufacturer	Webley & Scott Ltd, Birmingham
Original construction	1913
Calibre	·455 Webley
Ammunition reference	56-59
Number of rounds	6
Barrel length	152·2 mm
Weight unloaded	1055 g
Length, overall	281 mm
Height, overall	156 mm
Width, overall	44·3 mm
Sights	adjustable foresight
Safety	none
Metal finish	blued
Grip surface	vulcanized rubber
Breech/system	double-action
Inscription	WEBLEY MARK V PATENTS 1915

Manufacturer	Webley & Scott Ltd, Birmingham
Original construction	1915
Calibre	·455 Webley
Ammunition reference	56-59
Number of rounds	6
Barrel length	152·4 mm
Weight unloaded	1085 g
Length, overall	285 mm
Height, overall	157 mm
Width, overall	44·1 mm
Sights	fixed
Safety	none
Metal finish	blued
Grip surface	vulcanized rubber
Breech/system	double-action
Inscription	WEBLEY
	MARK VI
	PATENTS 1915

Manufacturer	Webley & Scott Ltd, Birmingham
Original construction	1915
Calibre	·455 Webley
Ammunition reference	56-59
Number of rounds	6
Barrel length	152·6 mm
Weight unloaded	1085 g
Length, overall	285 mm
Height, overall	157 mm
Width, overall	44·3 mm
Sights	adjustable foresight
Safety	none
Metal finish	blued
Grip surface	vulcanized rubber
Breech/system	double-action
Inscription	WEBLEY MARK VI PATENTS 1915

Part of shoulder stock is also shown

Manufacturer	Royal Small Arms Factory, Enfield
Original construction	1915
Calibre	·455 Webley
Ammunition reference	56-59
Number of rounds	6
Barrel length	152·2 mm
Weight unloaded	1075 g
Length, overall	286 mm
Height, overall	155 mm
Width, overall	44·3 mm
Sights	adjustable foresight
Safety	none
Metal finish	blued
Grip surface	vulcanized rubber
Breech/system	double-action
Inscription	WEBLEY
	MARK VI
	PATENTS 1925

Manufacturer	Webley & Scott Birmingham
Original construction	1929
Calibre	·38/200 ·38 S&W
Ammunition reference	42/43
Number of rounds	6
Barrel length	77 mm
Weight unloaded	610 g
Length, overall	184 mm
Height, overall	106 mm
Width, overall	36·9 mm
Sights	fixed
Safety	none
Metal finish	blued
Grip surface	vulcanized rubber
Breech/system	double-action
Inscription	MARK III ·38 WEBLEY & SCOTT LTD. BIRMINGHAM MADE IN ENGLAND

Manufacturer	Webley & Scott Ltd., Birmingham
Original construction	1929
Calibre	·38/200 ·38 S&W
Ammunition reference	42/43
Number of rounds	6
Barrel length	75·9 mm
Weight unloaded	750 g
Length, overall	205 mm
Height, overall	142 mm
Width, overall	36·9 mm
Sights	fixed
Safety	none
Metal finish	blued
Grip surface	vulcanized rubber
Breech/system	double-action
Inscription	MARK IV ·38 WEBLEY & SCOTT LTD. BIRMINGHAM MADE IN ENGLAND

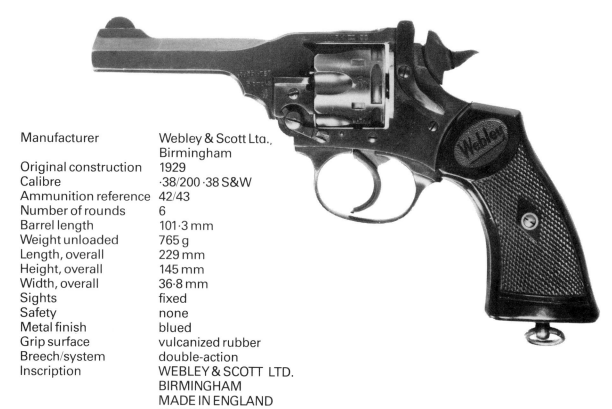

Manufacturer	Webley & Scott Ltd., Birmingham
Original construction	1929
Calibre	·38/200 ·38 S&W
Ammunition reference	42/43
Number of rounds	6
Barrel length	101·3 mm
Weight unloaded	765 g
Length, overall	229 mm
Height, overall	145 mm
Width, overall	36·8 mm
Sights	fixed
Safety	none
Metal finish	blued
Grip surface	vulcanized rubber
Breech/system	double-action
Inscription	WEBLEY & SCOTT LTD. BIRMINGHAM MADE IN ENGLAND MARK IV ·38

Manufacturer	Webley & Scott Ltd., Birmingham
Original construction	1929
Calibre	·38/200 ·38 S&W
Ammunition reference	42/43
Number of rounds	6
Barrel length	126·3 mm
Weight unloaded	810 g
Length, overall	256 mm
Height, overall	144 mm
Width, overall	36·8 mm
Sights	fixed
Safety	none
Metal finish	blued
Grip surface	vulcanized rubber
Breech/system	double-action
Inscription	MARK IV ·38 WEBLEY & SCOTT LTD. BIRMINGHAM MADE IN ENGLAND

149

Manufacturer	Webley & Scott Ltd., Birmingham
Original construction	1929
Calibre	·38/200 ·38 S&W
Ammunition reference	42/43
Number of rounds	6
Barrel length	126 mm
Weight unloaded	795 g
Length, overall	255 mm
Height, overall	147 mm
Width, overall	36·9 mm
Sights	fixed
Safety	none
Metal finish	blued
Grip surface	vulcanized rubber
Breech/system	double-action
Inscription	MARK IV ·38 WEBLEY & SCOTT LTD. WAR FINISH

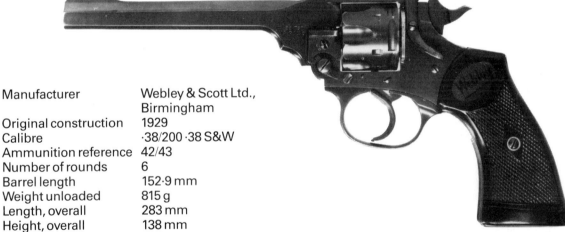

Manufacturer	Webley & Scott Ltd., Birmingham
Original construction	1929
Calibre	·38/200 ·38 S&W
Ammunition reference	42/43
Number of rounds	6
Barrel length	152·9 mm
Weight unloaded	815 g
Length, overall	283 mm
Height, overall	138 mm
Width, overall	36·8 mm
Sights	adjustable foresight
Safety	none
Metal finish	blued
Grip surface	vulcanized rubber
Breech/system	double-action
Inscription	MARK IV ·38
	WEBLEY & SCOTT LTD.
	BIRMINGHAM 4
	MADE IN ENGLAND

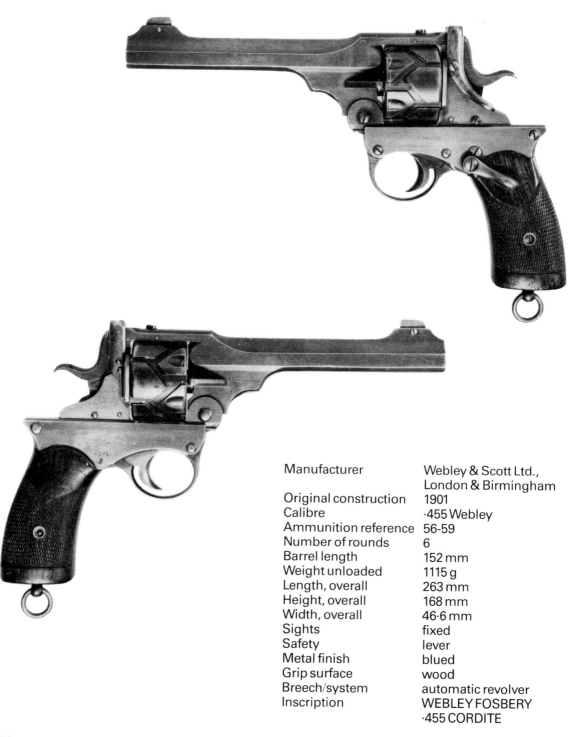

Manufacturer	Webley & Scott Ltd., London & Birmingham
Original construction	1901
Calibre	·455 Webley
Ammunition reference	56-59
Number of rounds	6
Barrel length	152 mm
Weight unloaded	1115 g
Length, overall	263 mm
Height, overall	168 mm
Width, overall	46·6 mm
Sights	fixed
Safety	lever
Metal finish	blued
Grip surface	wood
Breech/system	automatic revolver
Inscription	WEBLEY FOSBERY ·455 CORDITE

Manufacturer	Webley & Scott Ltd., London & Birmingham
Original construction	1901
Calibre	·455 Webley
Ammunition reference	56-59
Number of rounds	6
Barrel length	152 mm
Weight unloaded	1245 g
Length, overall	269 mm
Height, overall	181 mm
Width, overall	46·6 mm
Sights	fixed
Safety	lever
Metal finish	blued
Grip surface	vulcanized rubber
Breech/system	automatic revolver
Inscription	WEBLEY FOSBERY ·455 CORDITE

Manufacturer	Webley & Scott Ltd., London & Birmingham
Original construction	1901
Calibre	·455 Webley
Ammunition reference	56-59
Number of rounds	6
Barrel length	152 mm
Weight unloaded	1220 g
Length, overall	268 mm
Height, overall	176 mm
Width, overall	47·6 mm
Sights	fixed
Safety	lever
Metal finish	blued
Grip surface	wood
Breech/system	automatic revolver
Inscription	WEBLEY FOSBERY AUTOMATIC ·455 CORDITE ONLY

Webley & Scott ·38 Automatic Pistol

Manufacturer	Webley & Scott Ltd., Birmingham
Original construction	1909
Calibre	·38 Auto
Ammunition reference	45
Number of rounds	8
Barrel length	126.8 mm
Weight unloaded	975 g
Length, overall	216 mm
Height, overall	144 mm
Width, overall	35·5 mm
Sights	fixed
Safety	lever
Metal finish	blued
Grip surface	vulcanized rubber
Breech/system	locked
Inscription	WEBLEY & SCOTT LTD LONDON & BIRMINGHAM ·38 AUTOMATIC PISTOL

Webley & Scott 9mm Automatic Pistol

Manufacturer	Webley & Scott Ltd., Birmingham
Original construction	1909
Calibre	9 mm Browning Long
Ammunition reference	39
Number of rounds	8
Barrel length	126.8 mm
Weight unloaded	970 g
Length, overall	217·5 mm
Height, overall	141 mm
Width, overall	34·7 mm
Sights	fixed
Safety	grip
Metal finish	blued
Grip surface	wood
Breech/system	locked
Inscription	WEBLEY & SCOTT LTD LONDON & BIRMINGHAM 9 M/M AUTOMATIC PISTOL

UK

Webley & Scott 7·65 mm — ·32 Automatic Pistol

Manufacturer	Webley & Scott Ltd., Birmingham
Original construction	1913
Calibre	7·65 mm Browning
Ammunition reference	17
Number of rounds	8
Barrel length	88.6 mm
Weight unloaded	570 g
Length, overall	156 mm
Height, overall	115 mm
Width, overall	29·3 mm
Sights	fixed
Safety	lever
Metal finish	blued
Grip surface	vulcanized rubber
Breech/system	blowback
Inscription	WEBLEY & SCOTT LTD LONDON & BIRMINGHAM 7·65 M/M & ·32 AUTOMATIC PISTOL

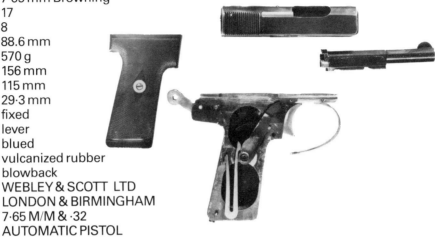

UK Webley & Scott Pistol Selfloading ·455 Mk I

Manufacturer	Webley & Scott Ltd., Birmingham
Original construction	1909/13
Calibre	·455 Webley Auto
Ammunition reference	60
Number of rounds	8
Barrel length	126.8 mm
Weight unloaded	1120 g
Length, overall	216 mm
Height, overall	148 mm
Width, overall	38·2 mm
Sights	fixed
Safety	grip
Metal finish	blued
Grip surface	vulcanized rubber
Breech/system	locked
Inscription	WEBLEY & SCOTT LTD PISTOL SELF-LOADING ·455 MARK I N 1917

UK

Welrod

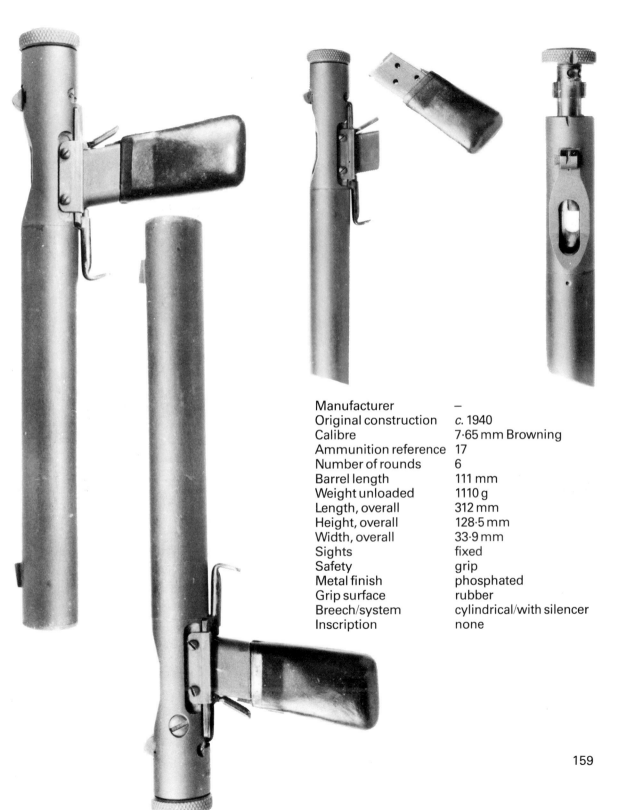

Manufacturer	–
Original construction	*c.* 1940
Calibre	7·65 mm Browning
Ammunition reference	17
Number of rounds	6
Barrel length	111 mm
Weight unloaded	1110 g
Length, overall	312 mm
Height, overall	128·5 mm
Width, overall	33·9 mm
Sights	fixed
Safety	grip
Metal finish	phosphated
Grip surface	rubber
Breech/system	cylindrical/with silencer
Inscription	none

HUNGARY

Frommer Mod. 1901/10

Manufacturer	Femaru Fegyver es Gepgyar
Original construction	1901
Calibre	7·65 mm Frommer
Ammunition reference	16
Number of rounds	8
Barrel length	119 mm
Weight unloaded	640 g
Length, overall	186 mm
Height, overall	127 mm
Width, overall	32 mm
Sights	fixed
Safety	grip
Metal finish	blued
Grip surface	wood
Breech/system	locked
Inscription	FEGYVERGYAR-BUDAPEST FROMMER-PAT.

Manufacturer	Fegyvergyar, Budapest
Original construction	1911
Calibre	7·65 mm Browning
Ammunition reference	17
Number of rounds	7
Barrel length	96 mm
Weight unloaded	595 g
Length, overall	165 mm
Height, overall	119 mm
Width, overall	27·3 mm
Sights	fixed
Safety	grip
Metal finish	blued
Grip surface	wood
Breech/system	locked
Inscription	FEGYVERGYAR-BUDAPEST FROMMER-PAT. STOP CAL. 7,65 MM (·32)

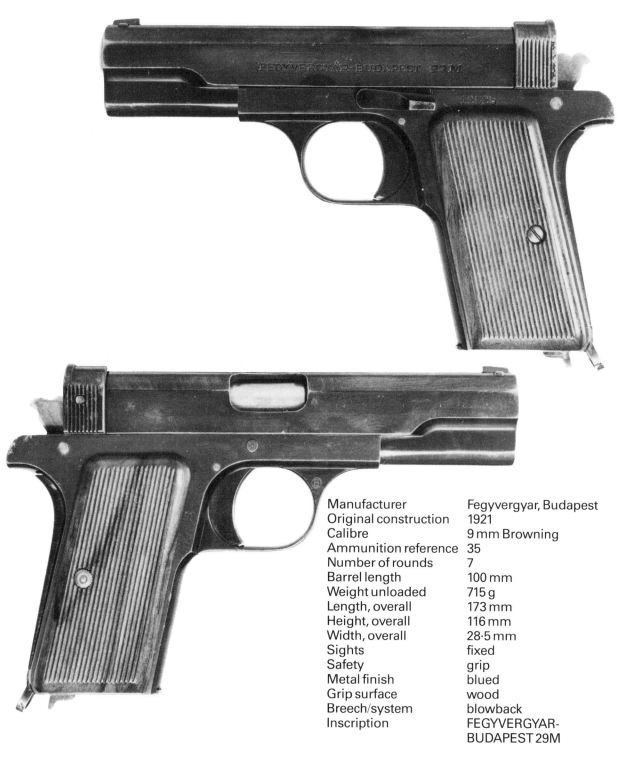

Manufacturer	Fegyvergyar, Budapest
Original construction	1921
Calibre	9 mm Browning
Ammunition reference	35
Number of rounds	7
Barrel length	100 mm
Weight unloaded	715 g
Length, overall	173 mm
Height, overall	116 mm
Width, overall	28·5 mm
Sights	fixed
Safety	grip
Metal finish	blued
Grip surface	wood
Breech/system	blowback
Inscription	FEGYVERGYAR-BUDAPEST 29M

Manufacturer	Femaru-Fegyvergyar (Arms and Machine Factory Co.)
Original construction	1937
Calibre	9 mm Browning
Ammunition reference	35
Number of rounds	7
Barrel length	100 mm
Weight unloaded	740 g
Length, overall	173 mm
Height, overall	128 mm
Width, overall	30·9 mm
Sights	fixed
Safety	grip
Metal finish	blued
Grip surface	wood
Breech/system	blowback
Inscription	FÉMÁRU-FEGYVER-ÉS GÉPGYAR P.T. 37 M

Manufacturer	unknown
Original construction	1930
Calibre	7·62 mm Tokarev
Ammunition reference	10
Number of rounds	8
Barrel length	115·8 mm
Weight unloaded	850 g
Length, overall	196 mm
Height, overall	135 mm
Width, overall	30·2 mm
Sights	fixed
Safety	none
Metal finish	blued
Grip surface	plastic
Breech/system	locked
Inscription	none

ITALY

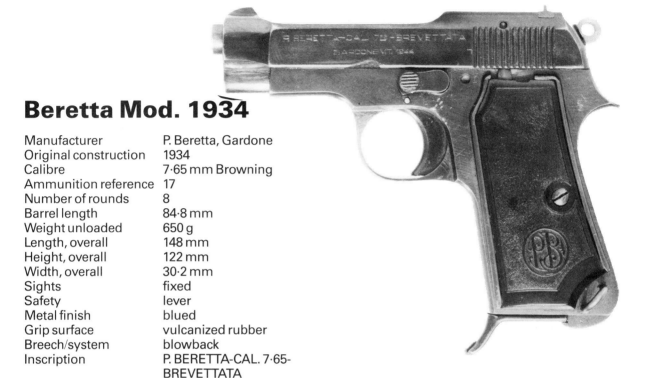

Beretta Mod. 1934

Manufacturer	P. Beretta, Gardone
Original construction	1934
Calibre	7·65 mm Browning
Ammunition reference	17
Number of rounds	8
Barrel length	84·8 mm
Weight unloaded	650 g
Length, overall	148 mm
Height, overall	122 mm
Width, overall	30·2 mm
Sights	fixed
Safety	lever
Metal finish	blued
Grip surface	vulcanized rubber
Breech/system	blowback
Inscription	P. BERETTA-CAL. 7·65-BREVETTATA GRADONE V.T.1944

Manufacturer	Metallurgica Brescia gia Temprini SA
Original construction	1906/09
Calibre	9 mm Glisenti
Ammunition reference	36
Number of rounds	8
Barrel length	94·5 mm
Weight unloaded	965 g
Length, overall	217 mm
Height, overall	146 mm
Width, overall	29·2 mm
Sights	fixed
Safety	lever
Metal finish	blued
Grip surface	vulcanized rubber
Breech/system	locked
Inscription	none

166

ITALY

Glisenti Mod. 1910

Manufacturer	Societa Siderugica Glisenti
Original construction	1906/09
Calibre	9 mm Glisenti
Ammunition reference	36
Number of rounds	7
Barrel length	95 mm
Weight unloaded	860 g
Length, overall	218 mm
Height, overall	146 mm
Width, overall	39·7 mm
Sights	fixed
Safety	lever
Metal finish	blued
Grip surface	vulcanized rubber
Breech/system	locked
Inscription	FAB 1910

JAPAN

Nambu (Papa Nambu)

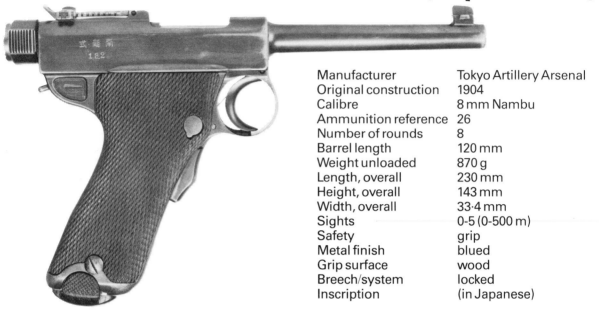

Manufacturer	Tokyo Artillery Arsenal
Original construction	1904
Calibre	8 mm Nambu
Ammunition reference	26
Number of rounds	8
Barrel length	120 mm
Weight unloaded	870 g
Length, overall	230 mm
Height, overall	143 mm
Width, overall	33·4 mm
Sights	0-5 (0-500 m)
Safety	grip
Metal finish	blued
Grip surface	wood
Breech/system	locked
Inscription	(in Japanese)

JAPAN

Nambu (Baby Nambu)

Manufacturer	Tokyo Artillery Arsenal
Original construction	1904
Calibre	7 mm Nambu
Ammunition reference	5
Number of rounds	7
Barrel length	83 mm
Weight unloaded	590 g
Length, overall	173 mm
Height, overall	114 mm
Width, overall	32·3 mm
Sights	fixed
Safety	grip
Metal finish	blued
Grip surface	wood
Breech/system	locked
Inscription	(in Japanese)

Manufacturer	Kokura Arsenal
Original construction	1925
Calibre	8 mm Nambu
Ammunition reference	26
Number of rounds	8
Barrel length	116·2 mm
Weight unloaded	910 g
Length, overall	233 mm
Height, overall	151 mm
Width, overall	33·1 mm
Sights	fixed
Safety	lever and magazine
Metal finish	blued
Grip surface	wood
Breech/system	locked
Inscription	(in Japanese)

170

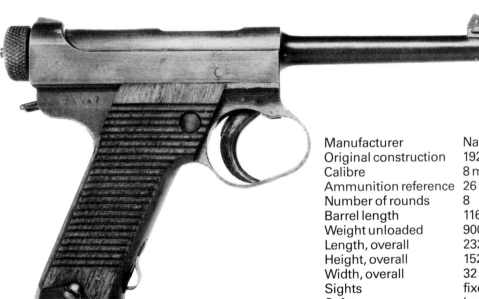

Manufacturer	Nagoya Arsenal
Original construction	1925
Calibre	8 mm Nambu
Ammunition reference	26
Number of rounds	8
Barrel length	116·3 mm
Weight unloaded	900 g
Length, overall	232 mm
Height, overall	152 mm
Width, overall	32 mm
Sights	fixed
Safety	lever and magazine
Metal finish	blued
Grip surface	wood
Breech/system	locked
Inscription	(in Japanese)

JAPAN   Nambu Type 94

Manufacturer	Nagoya Arsenal
Original construction	1934
Calibre	8 mm Nambu
Ammunition reference	26
Number of rounds	8
Barrel length	79 mm
Weight unloaded	770 g
Length, overall	154 mm
Height, overall	123 mm
Width, overall	26·9 mm
Sights	fixed
Safety	lever and magazine
Metal finish	blued
Grip surface	wood
Breech/system	blowback
Inscription	(in Japanese)

NORWAY

Norwegian Ordnance M 14

Manufacturer	Kongsberg Vapenfabrik, Kongsberg, Norway
Original construction	1911
Calibre	11·25 mm Norwegian Ordnance
Ammunition reference	50
Number of rounds	7
Barrel length	123·8 mm
Weight unloaded	1090 g
Length, overall	216 mm
Height, overall	144 mm
Width, overall	33 mm
Sights	fixed
Safety	lever and grip
Metal finish	blued
Grip surface	wood
Breech/system	locked
Inscription	11,25 m/m AUT. PISTOL M/1914 1924

Manufacturer	Kongsberg Vapenfabrik, Kongsberg, Norway
Original construction	1911
Calibre	11·25 mm Norwegian Ordnance
Ammunition reference	50
Number of rounds	7
Barrel length	123·9 mm
Weight unloaded	1095 g
Length, overall	216 mm
Height, overall	139 mm
Width, overall	32·8 mm
Sights	fixed
Safety	lever and grip
Metal finish	blued
Grip surface	plastic
Breech/system	locked
Inscription	11,25 m/m AUT.-PISTOL M/1914 1925

POLAND

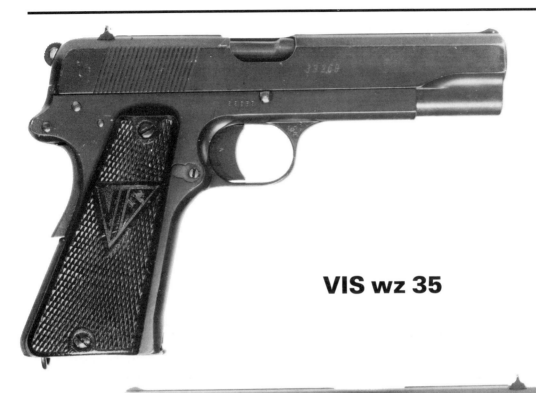

VIS wz 35

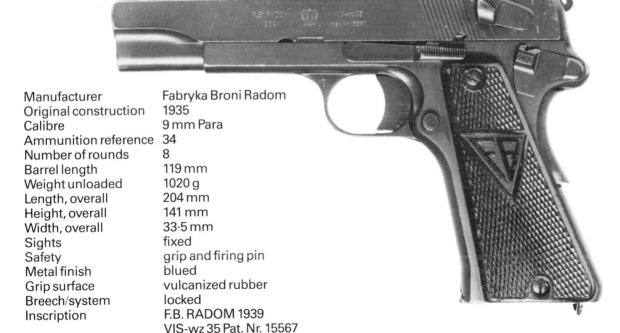

Manufacturer	Fabryka Broni Radom
Original construction	1935
Calibre	9 mm Para
Ammunition reference	34
Number of rounds	8
Barrel length	119 mm
Weight unloaded	1020 g
Length, overall	204 mm
Height, overall	141 mm
Width, overall	33·5 mm
Sights	fixed
Safety	grip and firing pin
Metal finish	blued
Grip surface	vulcanized rubber
Breech/system	locked
Inscription	F.B. RADOM 1939
	VIS-wz 35 Pat. Nr. 15567

Manufacturer	Fabryka Broni Radom
Original construction	1935
Calibre	9 mm Para
Ammunition reference	34
Number of rounds	8
Barrel length	119 mm
Weight unloaded	1010 g
Length, overall	206 mm
Height, overall	141 mm
Width, overall	33·3 mm
Sights	fixed
Safety	grip and firing pin
Metal finish	blued
Grip surface	vulcanized rubber
Breech/system	locked
Inscription	F.B. RADOM VIS Mod. 35 Pat. Nr. 15561 P. 35 (P)

POLAND

VIS wz 35

Manufacturer	Fabryka Broni Radom
Original construction	1935
Calibre	9 mm Para
Ammunition reference	34
Number of rounds	8
Barrel length	119 mm
Weight unloaded	1030 g
Length, overall	203 mm
Height, overall	144 mm
Width, overall	33·7 mm
Sights	fixed
Safety	grip and firing pin
Metal finish	blued
Grip surface	wood
Breech/system	locked
Inscription	F.B. RADOM VIS Mod. 35 Pat. Nr. 1556/7

PORTUGAL

Portuguese Ordnance revolver M 1878/86

Manufacturer	L. Soleil, Liège, Belgium	Width, overall	37·6 mm
Original construction	1878	Sights	fixed
Calibre	9·1 mm Abadie	Safety	none
Ammunition reference	41	Metal finish	blued
Number of rounds	6	Grip surface	wood
Barrel length	141·7 mm	Breech/system	double-action
Weight unloaded	845 g	Inscription	SYSTEM L. SOLEIL
Length, overall	250 mm		ABADIE F$^{\underline{T}}$
Height, overall	141 mm		BREVETE LIEGE

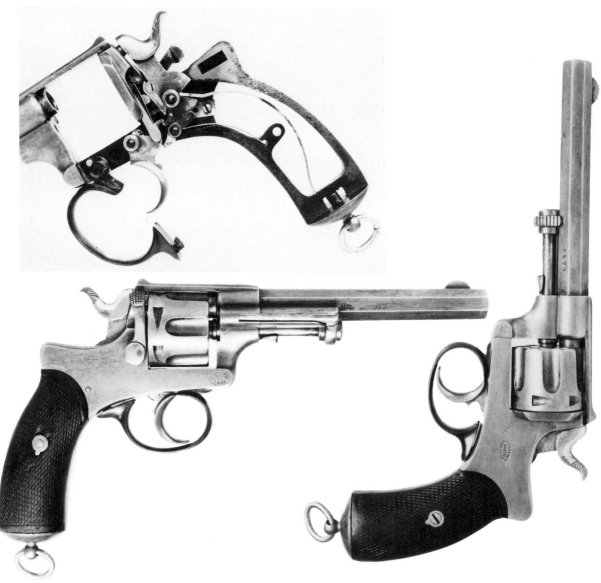

RUSSIA/SOVIET UNION

Nagant Mod. 1895

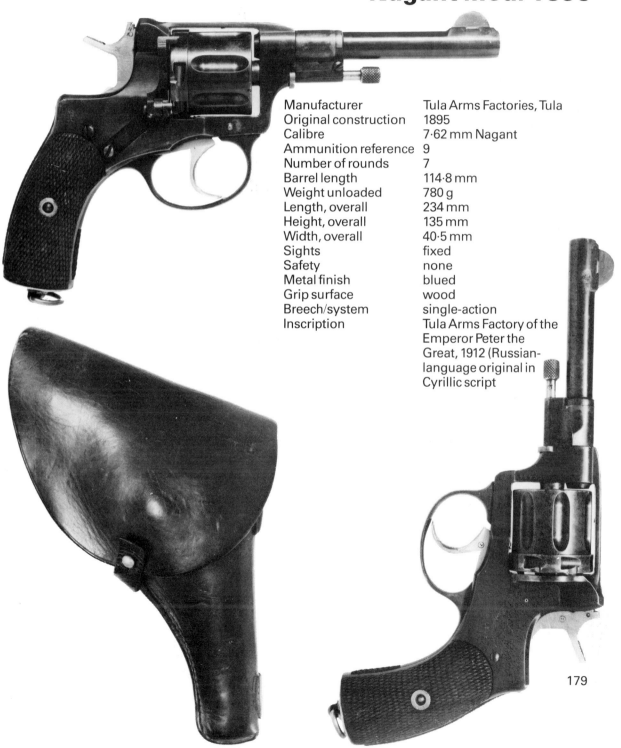

Manufacturer	Tula Arms Factories, Tula
Original construction	1895
Calibre	7·62 mm Nagant
Ammunition reference	9
Number of rounds	7
Barrel length	114·8 mm
Weight unloaded	780 g
Length, overall	234 mm
Height, overall	135 mm
Width, overall	40·5 mm
Sights	fixed
Safety	none
Metal finish	blued
Grip surface	wood
Breech/system	single-action
Inscription	Tula Arms Factory of the Emperor Peter the Great, 1912 (Russian-language original in Cyrillic script

Manufacturer	Soviet State armament factories
Original construction	1895
Calibre	7·62 mm Nagant
Ammunition reference	9
Number of rounds	7
Barrel length	114·1 mm
Weight unloaded	795 g
Length, overall	233 mm
Height, overall	134 mm
Width, overall	40·4 mm
Sights	fixed
Safety	none
Metal finish	blued
Grip surface	wood
Breech/system	double-action
Inscription	1938

SOVIET UNION

Nagant Mod. 1895

Manufacturer	Soviet State armament factories
Original construction	1895
Calibre	7·62 mm Nagant
Ammunition reference	9
Number of rounds	7
Barrel length	114·4 mm
Weight unloaded	800 g
Length, overall	233 mm
Height, overall	134 mm
Width, overall	40·3 mm
Sights	fixed
Safety	none
Metal finish	blued
Grip surface	wood
Breech/system	double-action
Inscription	1941

SOVIET UNION

Nagant Mod. 1895

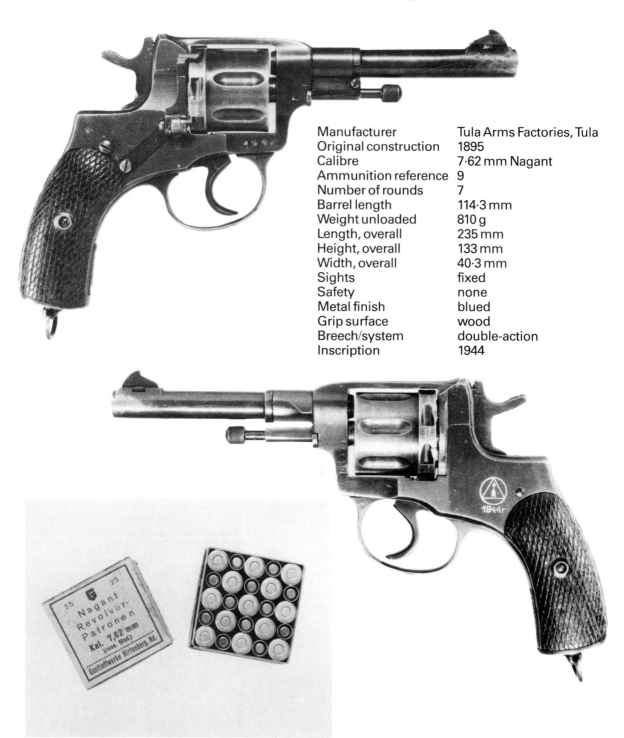

Manufacturer	Tula Arms Factories, Tula
Original construction	1895
Calibre	7·62 mm Nagant
Ammunition reference	9
Number of rounds	7
Barrel length	114·3 mm
Weight unloaded	810 g
Length, overall	235 mm
Height, overall	133 mm
Width, overall	40·3 mm
Sights	fixed
Safety	none
Metal finish	blued
Grip surface	wood
Breech/system	double-action
Inscription	1944

SOVIET UNION

Makarov

Manufacturer	Soviet State armament factories
Original construction	unknown
Calibre	9 mm Makarov
Ammunition reference	40
Number of rounds	8
Barrel length	93 mm
Weight unloaded	735 g
Length, overall	161 mm
Height, overall	126 mm
Width, overall	30·2 mm
Sights	fixed
Safety	lever
Metal finish	blued
Grip surface	plastic
Breech/system	blowback
Inscription	none

Manufacturer	Tula Arms Factories, Tula
Original construction	1930
Calibre	7·62 mm Tokarev
Ammunition reference	10
Number of rounds	8
Barrel length	115·7 mm
Weight unloaded	825 g
Length, overall	215 mm
Height, overall	132 mm
Width, overall	32·2 mm
Sights	fixed
Safety	none
Metal finish	blued
Grip surface	wood
Breech/system	locked
Inscription	Kh D 6777 1945 (in Cyrillic script)

SOVIET UNION

TK (Tulsky-Korovin)

Manufacturer	Tula Arms Factories, Tula
Original construction	1930
Calibre	6·35 mm Browning
Ammunition reference	3
Number of rounds	8
Barrel length	67·5 mm
Weight unloaded	395 g
Length, overall	127 mm
Height, overall	99 mm
Width, overall	24 mm
Sights	fixed
Safety	lever
Metal finish	blued
Grip surface	wood
Breech/system	blowback
Inscription	none

SPAIN

Alkar

Manufacturer	Manufacture de Armas de Fuego Guernica
Original construction	1910
Calibre	7·65 mm Browning
Ammunition reference	17
Number of rounds	9
Barrel length	127·3 mm
Weight unloaded	980 g
Length, overall	198 mm
Height, overall	129 mm
Width, overall	31·6 mm
Sights	fixed
Safety	lever
Metal finish	blued
Grip surface	wood
Breech/system	blowback
Inscription	S. A. ALKARTASUNA FABRICA DE ARMAS GUERNICA

SPAIN

Astra Mod. 200

Manufacturer	Astra-Unceta y Compania, Guernica
Original construction	1906
Calibre	6·35 mm Browning
Ammunition reference	3
Number of rounds	6
Barrel length	56·5 mm
Weight unloaded	355 g
Length, overall	110 mm
Height, overall	79 mm
Width, overall	23 mm
Sights	fixed
Safety	lever, magazine and grip
Metal finish	blued
Grip surface	vulcanized rubber
Breech/system	blowback
Inscription	Unceta y Compania S.A. Guernica ASTRA-CAL. 6,35 ·25 MADE IN SPAIN

Manufacturer	Astra-Unceta y Compania, Guernica
Original construction	1921
Calibre	9 mm Browning
Ammunition reference	35
Number of rounds	7
Barrel length	99·1 mm
Weight unloaded	635 g
Length, overall	160 mm
Height, overall	108 mm
Width, overall	30 mm
Sights	fixed
Safety	lever, magazine and grip
Metal finish	blued
Grip surface	wood
Breech/system	blowback
Inscription	UNCETA Y COMPAÑIA GUERNICA ESPAÑA

SPAIN

Astra Mod. 600/43 Chile

Manufacturer	Astra-Unceta y Compania, Guernica
Original construction	1921
Calibre	9 mm Para
Ammunition reference	34
Number of rounds	8
Barrel length	134·3 mm
Weight unloaded	990 g
Length, overall	205 mm
Height, overall	133 mm
Width, overall	30 mm
Sights	fixed
Safety	lever, magazine and grip
Metal finish	blued
Grip surface	wood
Breech/system	blowback
Inscription	UNCETA Y COMPAÑIA S.A. GUERNICA ESPAÑA ASTRA MOD. 600/43 9 mm Parabellum Made in Spain FUERZA AEREA DE CHILE

Manufacturer	Astra-Unceta y Compania, Guernica
Original construction	1921
Calibre	9 mm Para
Ammunition reference	34
Number of rounds	8
Barrel length	134·2 mm
Weight unloaded	1000 g
Length, overall	205 mm
Height, overall	129 mm
Width, overall	30·2 mm
Sights	fixed
Safety	lever, magazine and grip
Metal finish	blued
Grip surface	wood
Breech/system	blowback
Inscription	UNCETA Y COMPAÑIA S.A. GUERNICA ESPAÑA "ASTRA" MOD. 600/43 9 mm Parabellum Made in Spain

Astra Mod. F

Manufacturer	Astra-Unceta y Compania, Guernica
Original construction	1926
Calibre	9 mm Largo
Ammunition reference	33
Number of rounds	10 and 20
Barrel length	160·2 mm
Weight unloaded	1470 g
Length, overall	314 mm
Height, overall	158 mm
Width, overall	37·5 mm
Sights	50-500 m
Safety	lever
Metal finish	blued
Grip surface	wood
Breech/system	locked
Inscription	Pist.^{a} Ametr.^{a} ASTRA mod^{o} F de 9 mm (·38) UNCETA Y COMPAÑIA GUERNICA ESPAÑA

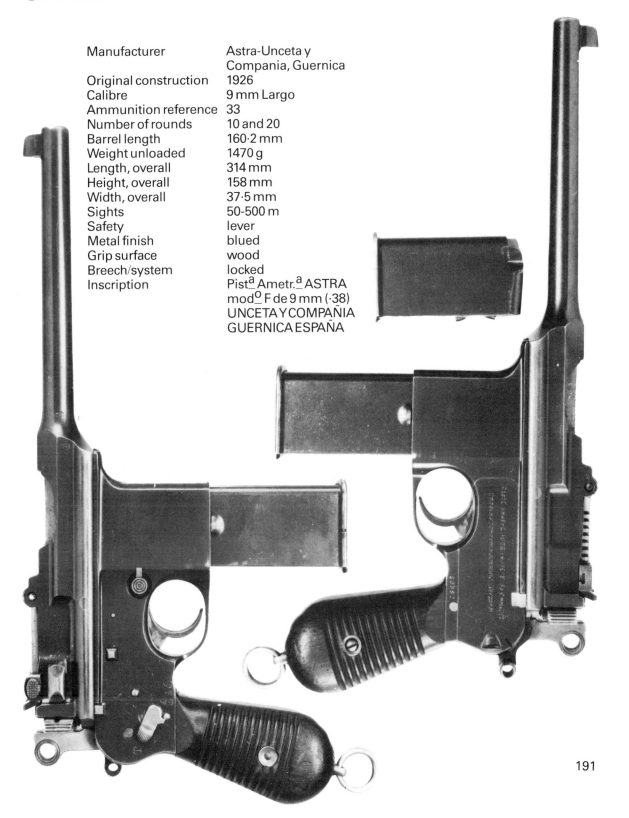

SPAIN

Azul Mod. 1931

Manufacturer	Eulogio y Compania, Eibar
Original construction	1931
Calibre	9 mm Largo
Ammunition reference	33
Number of rounds	20
Barrel length	180·5 mm
Weight unloaded	1550 g
Length, overall	336·5 mm
Height, overall	163 mm
Width, overall	38 mm
Sights	adjustable 50-1000 m
Safety	lever
Metal finish	blued
Grip surface	wood
Breech/system	locked
Inscription	MM 31

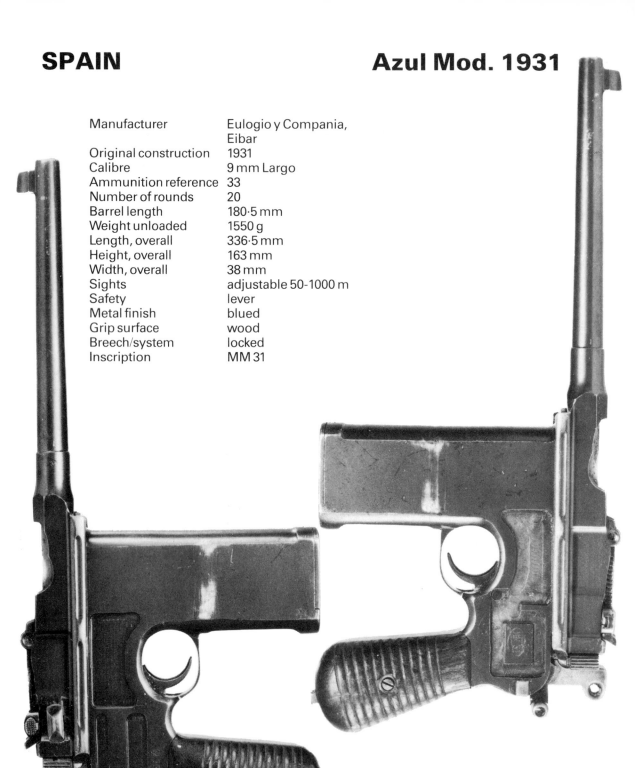

SPAIN   Campo Giro Mod. 13-16

Manufacturer	Esperanza Unceta, Guernica
Original construction	1904
Calibre	9 mm Largo
Ammunition reference	33
Number of rounds	8
Barrel length	167·5 mm
Weight unloaded	1030 g
Length, overall	243 mm
Height, overall	137 mm
Width, overall	33 mm
Sights	fixed
Safety	lever
Metal finish	blued
Grip surface	wood
Breech/system	blowback
Inscription	CAMPO-GIRO PAT. 34798-54214 1904-1913 Pist.ª Aut.ª mod. 1913-16 ESPERANZA Y UNCETA GUERNICA

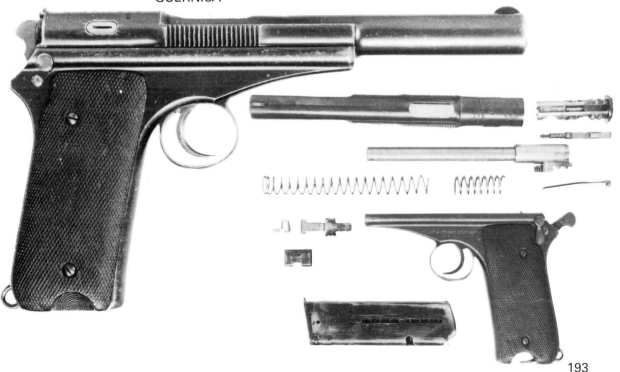

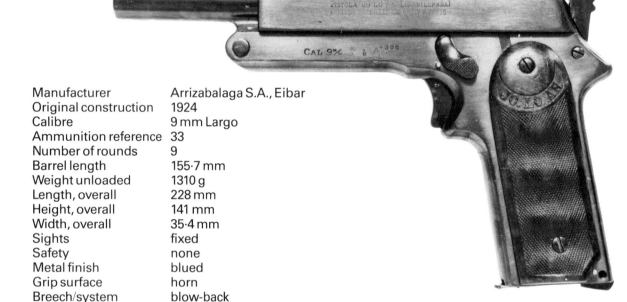

Manufacturer	Arrizabalaga S.A., Eibar
Original construction	1924
Calibre	9 mm Largo
Ammunition reference	33
Number of rounds	9
Barrel length	155·7 mm
Weight unloaded	1310 g
Length, overall	228 mm
Height, overall	141 mm
Width, overall	35·4 mm
Sights	fixed
Safety	none
Metal finish	blued
Grip surface	horn
Breech/system	blow-back
Inscription	PISTOLA "JO-LO-AR"
	EIBAR (ESPAÑA)
	68027 y 70235
	JO-LO-AR E CAL. 9 m/m

Manufacturer	Bonifacio Echeverria y Cia, Eibar
Original construction	1914
Calibre	7·65 mm Browning
Ammunition reference	17
Number of rounds	9
Barrel length	97 mm
Weight unloaded	790 g
Length, overall	163 mm
Height, overall	119 mm
Width, overall	28·9 mm
Sights	fixed
Safety	lever
Metal finish	blued
Grip surface	vulcanized rubber
Breech/system	blowback
Inscription	AUTOMATIC PISTOL "STAR" CAL. 32

Manufacturer	Bonifacio Echeverria y Cia, Eibar
Original construction	1914
Calibre	7·65 mm Browning
Ammunition reference	17
Number of rounds	9
Barrel length	127·5 mm
Weight unloaded	750 g
Length, overall	202 mm
Height, overall	123 mm
Width, overall	30·5 mm
Sights	fixed
Safety	lever
Metal finish	blued
Grip surface	wood
Breech/system	blowback
Inscription	CAL. 7,^{65}

Manufacturer	Ruby Arms Co., Guernica
Original construction	1915
Calibre	7·65 mm Browning
Ammunition reference	17
Number of rounds	9
Barrel length	88·4 mm
Weight unloaded	785 g
Length, overall	154 mm
Height, overall	127 mm
Width, overall	34·4 mm
Sights	fixed
Safety	lever
Metal finish	blued
Grip surface	wood
Breech/system	blowback
Inscription	1915 PATENT "RUBY" CAL. 7,$\frac{65}{}$

SPAIN   Ruby Type pistol

Manufacturer	unknown
Original construction	1914
Calibre	7·65 mm Browning
Ammunition reference	17
Number of rounds	9
Barrel length	84·3 mm
Weight unloaded	800 g
Length, overall	153 mm
Height, overall	128 mm
Width, overall	30 mm
Sights	fixed
Safety	lever
Metal finish	blued
Grip surface	vulcanized rubber
Breech/system	blowback
Inscription	7,$\frac{65}{}$1914 AUTOMATIC PISTOL "MILITARY"

SWEDEN

Husqvarna Mod. 1907

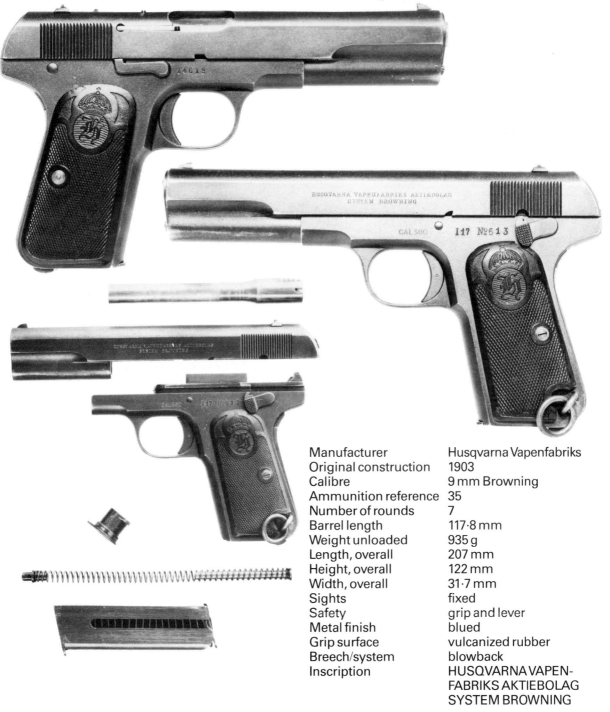

Manufacturer	Husqvarna Vapenfabriks
Original construction	1903
Calibre	9 mm Browning
Ammunition reference	35
Number of rounds	7
Barrel length	117·8 mm
Weight unloaded	935 g
Length, overall	207 mm
Height, overall	122 mm
Width, overall	31·7 mm
Sights	fixed
Safety	grip and lever
Metal finish	blued
Grip surface	vulcanized rubber
Breech/system	blowback
Inscription	HUSQVARNA VAPEN-FABRIKS AKTIEBOLAG SYSTEM BROWNING

SWEDEN   Norwegian Ordnance M 1887

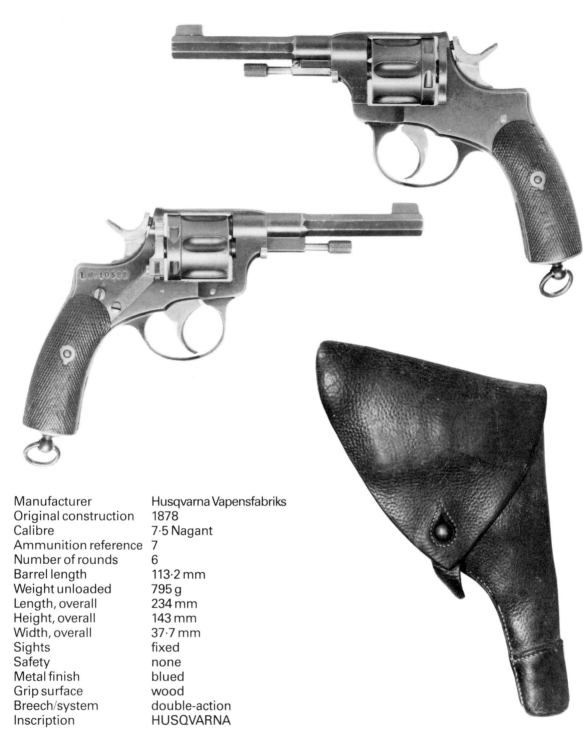

Manufacturer	Husqvarna Vapensfabriks
Original construction	1878
Calibre	7·5 Nagant
Ammunition reference	7
Number of rounds	6
Barrel length	113·2 mm
Weight unloaded	795 g
Length, overall	234 mm
Height, overall	143 mm
Width, overall	37·7 mm
Sights	fixed
Safety	none
Metal finish	blued
Grip surface	wood
Breech/system	double-action
Inscription	HUSQVARNA

SWEDEN   Swedish Ordnance Pistol M 40

Manufacturer	Husqvarna Vapensfabriks A.B.
Original construction	1935
Calibre	9 mm Para
Ammunition reference	34
Number of rounds	7
Barrel length	120·1 mm
Weight unloaded	1265 g
Length, overall	243 mm
Height, overall	146 mm
Width, overall	34·6 mm
Sights	fixed
Safety	lever
Metal finish	blued
Grip surface	vulcanized-rubber
Breech/system	locked
Inscription	HUSQVARNA VAPENFABRIKS A.B.

SWITZERLAND

Swiss Ordnance Mod. 1882

Manufacturer	Waffenfabrik Bern
Original construction	1882
Calibre	7·5 mm Swiss Ordnance
Ammunition reference	8
Number of rounds	6
Barrel length	115·4 mm
Weight unloaded	810 g
Length, overall	234 mm
Height, overall	134 mm
Width, overall	37·8 mm
Sights	fixed
Safety	none
Metal finish	blued
Grip surface	vulcanized rubber
Breech/system	double-action
Inscription	none

SWITZERLAND   Swiss Ordnance Mod. 1882

Manufacturer	Waffenfabrik Bern
Original construction	1882
Calibre	7·5 mm Swiss Ordnance
Ammunition reference	8
Number of rounds	6
Barrel length	116·1 mm
Weight unloaded	810 g
Length, overall	234 mm
Height, overall	136 mm
Width, overall	37·8 mm
Sights	fixed
Safety	none
Metal finish	blued
Grip surface	wood
Breech/system	double-action
Inscription	none

Manufacturer	Waffenfabrik Bern
Original construction	1882
Calibre	7·5 mm Swiss Ordnance
Ammunition reference	8
Number of rounds	6
Barrel length	114·6 mm
Weight unloaded	770 g
Length, overall	228 mm
Height, overall	139 mm
Width, overall	37·7 mm
Sights	fixed
Safety	none
Metal finish	blued
Grip surface	bakelite
Breech/system	double-action
Inscription	none

SWITZERLAND   Swiss Ordnance Mod. 00

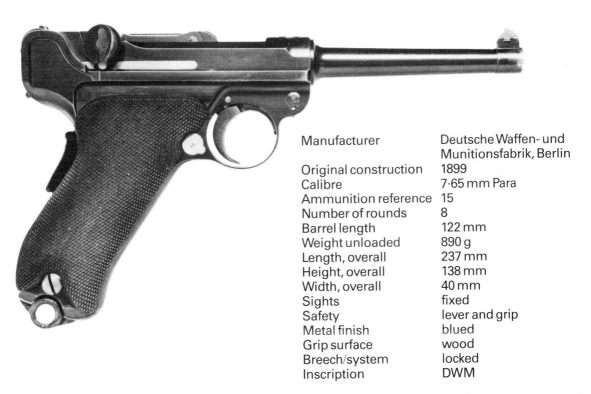

Manufacturer	Deutsche Waffen- und Munitionsfabrik, Berlin
Original construction	1899
Calibre	7·65 mm Para
Ammunition reference	15
Number of rounds	8
Barrel length	122 mm
Weight unloaded	890 g
Length, overall	237 mm
Height, overall	138 mm
Width, overall	40 mm
Sights	fixed
Safety	lever and grip
Metal finish	blued
Grip surface	wood
Breech/system	locked
Inscription	DWM

Manufacturer	Deutsche Waffen- und Munitionsfabrik, Berlin
Original construction	1899
Calibre	7·65 mm Para
Ammunition reference	15
Number of rounds	8
Barrel length	118 mm
Weight unloaded	890 g
Length, overall	234 mm
Height, overall	139 mm
Width, overall	39·5 mm
Sights	fixed
Safety	lever and grip
Metal finish	blued
Grip surface	wood
Breech/system	locked
Inscription	DWM

SWITZERLAND   Swiss Ordnance Mod. 29

Manufacturer	Waffenfabrik Bern
Original construction	1899
Calibre	7·65 mm Para
Ammunition reference	15
Number of rounds	8
Barrel length	120 mm
Weight unloaded	935 g
Length, overall	239 mm
Height, overall	138 mm
Width, overall	36 mm
Sights	fixed
Safety	lever and grip
Metal finish	blued
Grip surface	Canevasit (Swiss trade name)
Breech/system	locked
Inscription	none

Manufacturer	Schweizer Industrie-gesellschaft, Neuhausen
Original construction	1944
Calibre	9 mm Para
Ammunition reference	34
Number of rounds	8
Barrel length	120·4 mm
Weight unloaded	900 g
Length, overall	213 mm
Height, overall	138 mm
Width, overall	35 mm
Sights	fixed
Safety	lever
Metal finish	blued
Grip surface	wood
Breech/system	locked
Inscription	Schweizerische Industrie-Gesellschaft Neuhausen a./"Rhf"

SWITZERLAND

SIG SP 47/8

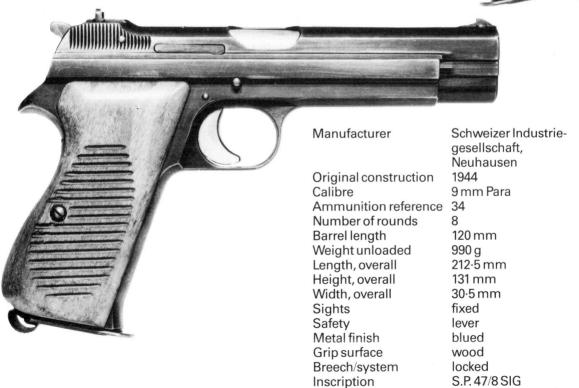

Manufacturer	Schweizer Industrie-gesellschaft, Neuhausen
Original construction	1944
Calibre	9 mm Para
Ammunition reference	34
Number of rounds	8
Barrel length	120 mm
Weight unloaded	990 g
Length, overall	212·5 mm
Height, overall	131 mm
Width, overall	30·5 mm
Sights	fixed
Safety	lever
Metal finish	blued
Grip surface	wood
Breech/system	locked
Inscription	S.P. 47/8 SIG

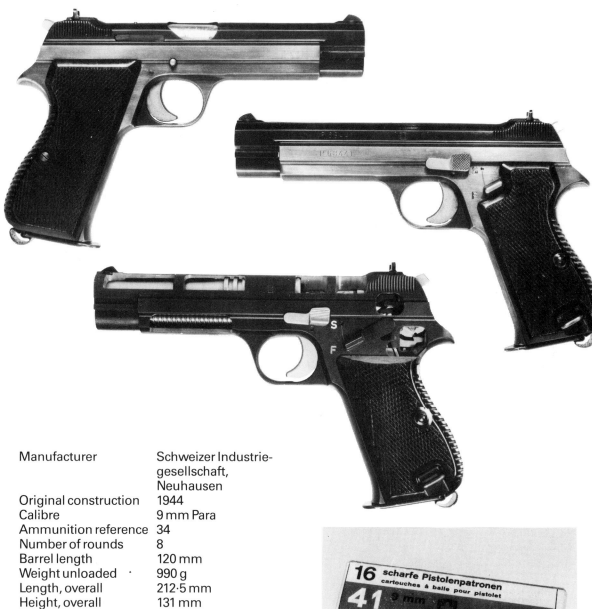

Manufacturer	Schweizer Industrie-gesellschaft, Neuhausen
Original construction	1944
Calibre	9 mm Para
Ammunition reference	34
Number of rounds	8
Barrel length	120 mm
Weight unloaded ·	990 g
Length, overall	212·5 mm
Height, overall	131 mm
Width, overall	30·5 mm
Sights	fixed
Safety	lever
Metal finish	blued
Grip surface	plastic
Breech/system	locked
Inscription	SIG

16 scharfe Pistolenpatronen
cartouches à balle pour pistolet

41 9 mm 15. 8. 55 T

Manufacturer	Schweizer Industrie-gesellschaft, Neuhausen
Original construction	1944
Calibre	9 mm Para
Ammunition reference	34
Number of rounds	8
Barrel length	120 mm
Weight unloaded	995 g
Length, overall	213 mm
Height, overall	131 mm
Width, overall	30·5 mm
Sights	fixed
Safety	lever
Metal finish	blued
Grip surface	plastic
Breech/system	locked
Inscription	SIG

USA

Colt Mod. 1911 A1

Manufacturer	Colt, Hartford, USA
Original construction	1911
Calibre	·45 ACP
Ammunition reference	55
Number of rounds	7
Barrel length	123·7 mm
Weight unloaded	1120 g
Length, overall	217 mm
Height, overall	137 mm
Width, overall	32 mm
Sights	fixed
Safety	lever and grip
Metal finish	phosphated
Grip surface	plastic
Breech/system	locked
Inscription	PATENTED APR.20.1897, SEPT.9.1902, DEC.19. 1905, FEB.14.1911, AUG.19.1913, COLT'S PT.FA.MFG.CO HARTFORD.CT.U.S.A. UNITED STATES PROPERTY M1911A1 U.S. ARMY

Manufacturer	Colt, Hartford, USA
Calibre	·38 Special
Ammunition reference	44
Number of rounds	6
Barrel length	100·9 mm
Weight unloaded	665 g
Length, overall	224 mm
Height, overall	126 mm
Width, overall	35·6 mm
Sights	fixed
Safety	none
Metal finish	blued
Grip surface	plastic
Breech/system	double-action
Inscription	POLICE POSITIVE SPECIAL ·38 SPECIAL CTG COLT'S MFG CO. HARTFORD CT U.S.A.

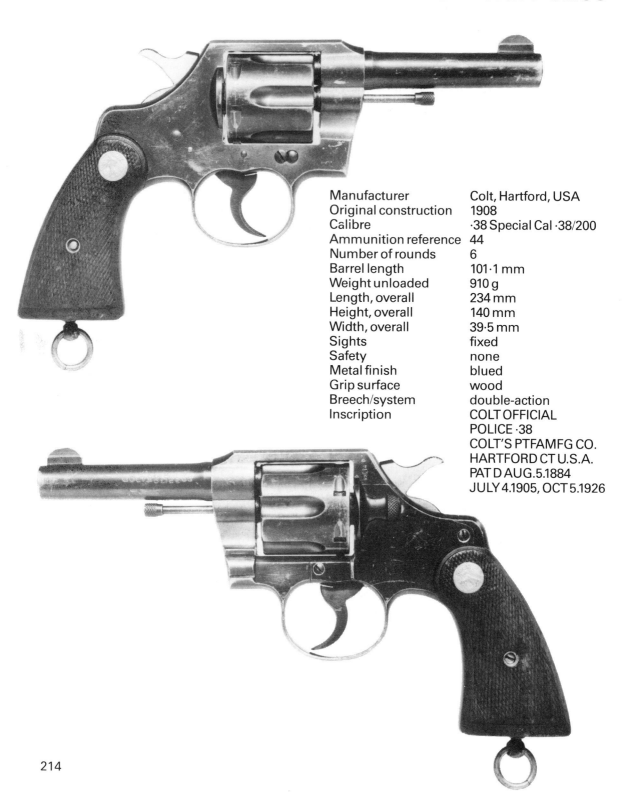

Manufacturer	Colt, Hartford, USA
Original construction	1908
Calibre	·38 Special Cal ·38/200
Ammunition reference	44
Number of rounds	6
Barrel length	101·1 mm
Weight unloaded	910 g
Length, overall	234 mm
Height, overall	140 mm
Width, overall	39·5 mm
Sights	fixed
Safety	none
Metal finish	blued
Grip surface	wood
Breech/system	double-action
Inscription	COLT OFFICIAL POLICE ·38 COLT'S PTFA MFG CO. HARTFORD CT U.S.A. PAT D AUG. 5. 1884 JULY 4. 1905, OCT 5. 1926

Manufacturer	Harrington & Richardson Arms Co., Worcester, Mass., USA
Original construction	1907
Calibre	·32 ACP
Ammunition reference	17
Number of rounds	8
Barrel length	89 mm
Weight unloaded	620 g
Length, overall	165 mm
Height, overall	118 mm
Width, overall	37·5 mm
Sights	fixed
Safety	lever and grip
Metal finish	blued
Grip surface	vulcanized rubber
Breech/system	blowback
Inscription	H. & R. SELF-LOADING CALIBER 32 HARRINGTON & RICHARDSON ARMS CO., WORCESTER, MASSACHUSETTS U.S.A. PAT. AUG.20.1907, APR.13, NOV.9.1909

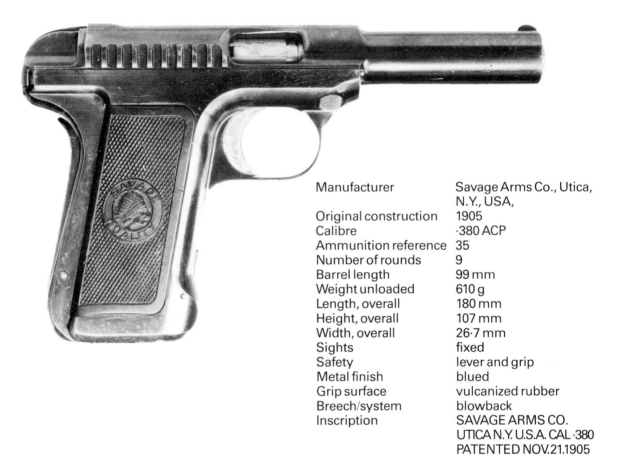

Manufacturer	Savage Arms Co., Utica, N.Y., USA,
Original construction	1905
Calibre	·380 ACP
Ammunition reference	35
Number of rounds	9
Barrel length	99 mm
Weight unloaded	610 g
Length, overall	180 mm
Height, overall	107 mm
Width, overall	26·7 mm
Sights	fixed
Safety	lever and grip
Metal finish	blued
Grip surface	vulcanized rubber
Breech/system	blowback
Inscription	SAVAGE ARMS CO. UTICA N.Y. U.S.A. CAL ·380 PATENTED NOV. 21.1905

Manufacturer	Savage Arms Co., Utica, N.Y., USA,
Original construction	1905
Calibre	·32 ACP
Ammunition reference	17
Number of rounds	10
Barrel length	96 mm
Weight unloaded	620 g
Length, overall	167 mm
Height, overall	108 mm
Width, overall	28·7 mm
Sights	fixed
Safety	lever
Metal finish	blued
Grip surface	vulcanized rubber
Breech/system	blowback
Inscription	SAVAGE ARMS CORP. UTICA N.Y. U.S.A. CAL ·32 PATENTED NOVEMBER 21.1905-7, 65 MM SAVAGE 1917 MODEL

Manufacturer	Smith & Wesson, Springfield, Mass., USA
Original construction	1899
Calibre	·38 S&W ·38/200
Ammunition reference	42/43
Number of rounds	6
Barrel length	126·5 mm
Weight unloaded	850 g
Length, overall	256 mm
Height, overall	139 mm
Width, overall	36·6 mm
Sights	fixed
Safety	none
Metal finish	blued
Grip surface	wood
Breech/system	double-action
Inscription	SMITH & WESSON
	·38 S&W CTG
	SMITH & WESSON
	SPRINGFIELD
	MASS. U.S.A.
	PATENTED FEB.6.06.
	SEPT.14.09. DEC.29.14.

USA Smith & Wesson M&P Mod. 1905

Manufacturer	Smith & Wesson, Springfield, Mass., USA
Original construction	1899
Calibre	·38 S&W ·38/200
Ammunition reference	42/43
Number of rounds	6
Barrel length	126·6 mm
Weight unloaded	855 g
Length, overall	256 mm
Height, overall	140 mm
Width, overall	36·6 mm
Sights	fixed
Safety	none
Metal finish	blued
Grip surface	wood
Breech/system	double-action
Inscription	SMITH & WESSON SPRINGFIELD MASS. U.S.A. PATENTED FEB.6.06, SEPT.14.09, DEC.29.14.

Smith & Wesson M&P Mod. 1905

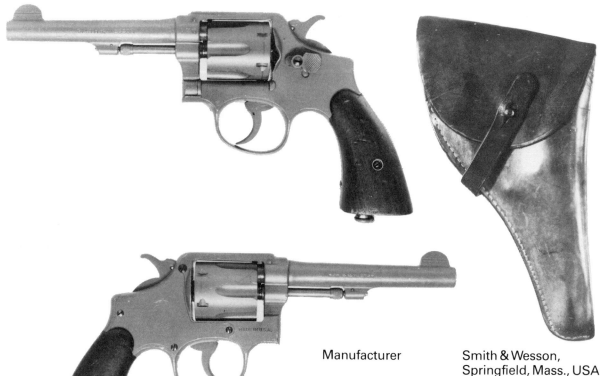

Manufacturer	Smith & Wesson, Springfield, Mass., USA
Original construction	1899
Calibre	·38 S&W ·38/200
Ammunition reference	42/43
Number of rounds	6
Barrel length	126·4 mm
Weight unloaded	845 g
Length, overall	258 mm
Height, overall	134 mm
Width, overall	36·8 mm
Sights	fixed
Safety	none
Metal finish	Parkerized
Grip surface	wood
Breech/system	double-action
Inscription	SMITH & WESSON UNITED STATES PROPERTY ·38 S&W CTG SMITH & WESSON SPRINGFIELD MASS. U.S.A. PATENTED FEB.6.06, SEPT.14.09, DEC.29.14. MADE IN U.S.A.

Smith & Wesson M&P Mod. 1905

Manufacturer	Smith & Wesson, Springfield, Mass., USA
Original construction	1899
Calibre	·38 S&W ·38/200
Ammunition reference	42/43
Number of rounds	6
Barrel length	152·3 mm
Weight unloaded	880 g
Length, overall	280 mm
Height, overall	141 mm
Width, overall	36·7 mm
Sights	fixed
Safety	none
Metal finish	blued
Grip surface	wood
Breech/system	double-action
Inscription	SMITH & WESSON 38 S&W CTG SMITH & WESSON SPRINGFIELD MASS. U.S.A. PATENTED FEB.6.06, SEPT.14.09, DEC.29.14.

USA   Smith & Wesson Russian

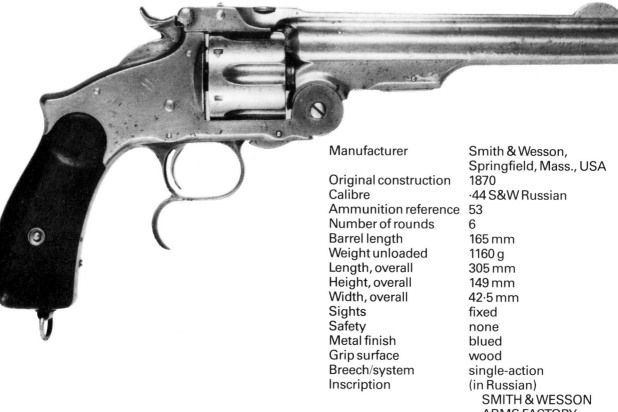

Manufacturer	Smith & Wesson, Springfield, Mass., USA
Original construction	1870
Calibre	·44 S&W Russian
Ammunition reference	53
Number of rounds	6
Barrel length	165 mm
Weight unloaded	1160 g
Length, overall	305 mm
Height, overall	149 mm
Width, overall	42·5 mm
Sights	fixed
Safety	none
Metal finish	blued
Grip surface	wood
Breech/system	single-action
Inscription	(in Russian)
	SMITH & WESSON
	ARMS FACTORY
	SPRINGFIELD
	AMERICA

USA   Smith & Wesson Russian

Manufacturer	Smith & Wesson, Springfield, Mass., USA
Original construction	1870
Calibre	·44 S&W Russian
Ammunition reference	53
Number of rounds	6
Barrel length	122 mm
Weight unloaded	1055 g
Length, overall	261 mm
Height, overall	148 mm
Width, overall	42·5 mm
Sights	fixed
Safety	none
Metal finish	blued
Grip surface	wood
Breech/system	single-action
Inscription	none

YUGOSLAVIA

Yovanovitch Mod. 1931

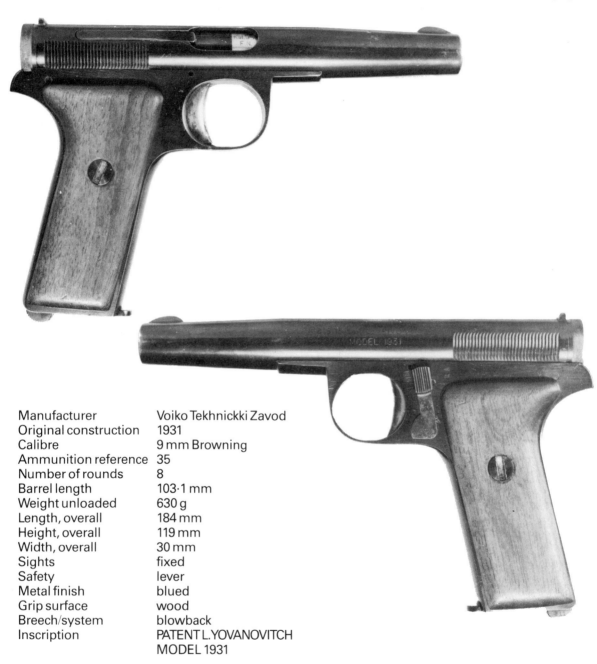

Manufacturer	Voiko Tekhnickki Zavod
Original construction	1931
Calibre	9 mm Browning
Ammunition reference	35
Number of rounds	8
Barrel length	103·1 mm
Weight unloaded	630 g
Length, overall	184 mm
Height, overall	119 mm
Width, overall	30 mm
Sights	fixed
Safety	lever
Metal finish	blued
Grip surface	wood
Breech/system	blowback
Inscription	PATENT L. YOVANOVITCH
	MODEL 1931

Cartridges

1. ·22 Long Rifle

A development of the ·22 Long cartridge by J. Stevens Arms & Tool Company. It has the same case but a longer bullet weighing approx 2·5 g which in the original version was propelled by 0·3 g of black powder. At that time it was known as 'Special ·22 Long Cartridge for rifle use' and was intended to be fired from long-barrelled rifles only. Nowadays this cartridge is of course loaded with smokeless powder and produced all over the world. Probably no other cartridge has found such widespread application. It is used for sport, hunting and self-defence, with only minor differences in the manufacturing process. It has hardly any military significance, apart from being used as training rounds for small calibre weapons or as sub-calibre liners for larger-calibre weapons.

Over the years the ·22 Long Rifle cartridge has undergone a steady development, including the introduction of erosion-proof primers and metallic jackets for its bullets which are intended to prevent premature lead deposits in the barrel.

Depending on the manufacturer, powder charge and the length of the barrel, the ·22 Long Rifle has a muzzle velocity of 330-450 m/sec.

2. 5 mm Bergmann No. 2 M 96

This cartridge replaced the No. 2 M 94 (bottle-necked case, without extractor rim) and differed from its predecessor solely by having the latter. It was intended for the Bergmann pocket pistols No. 1 and No. 2 and carries the same designation as the relevant weapons, M 96. It was manufactured by DWM until about 1930. (The early Bergmann pistols No. 1 and No. 2 were the only self-loading weapons using cartridges without extractor rim or groove, relying entirely on the residual chamber pressure to blow out the empty case when the breech was opened – unique, but not really successful. *Tr*)

Bullet diameter	5·20 – 5·25 mm
Case length	14·80 – 15·20 mm
Case material	brass
Propellant	smokeless
Priming	Berdan
Round length	21·00 – 22·50 mm
Muzzle velocity	180 m/sec
Muzzle energy	86·30 J
Length of test barrel	80 mm

3. 6·35 mm Browning

The 6·35 mm Browning was developed and introduced in 1906 by the Belgian firm of Fabrique Nationale d'Armes de Guerre at Herstal for their pocket pistol Model 1906. Later on, the same cartridge was manufactured by Colt in the USA under the designation ·25 Automatic (6·35 mm ACP) for their own pocket pistols. Since then this cartridge has found widespread use, and a number of small pocket pistols were developed to fire it. In fact, the 6.35 mm became *the* cartridge for pocket pistols. In its ballistic as well as its actual shooting performance when fired from short-barrelled weapons the effect of the 6·35 mm cartridge remains disputed, especially at the present time when more powerful cartridges can be fired from relatively small self-loading pistols.

Bullet diameter	6·30 – 6·39 mm
Case length	15·27 – 15·70 mm
Case material	brass
Propellant	smokeless
Priming	Berdan or Boxer
Round length	22·50 – 23·00 mm
Muzzle velocity	230 m/sec
Muzzle energy	86.30 J
Length of test barrel	80 mm

4. 6·5 mm Bergmann No. 3 M 96

Featured similar changes as to the 5 mm Bergmann cartridge: the bottle-necked M 94 without the extractor rim modified to have one. This extractor rim was essential because an improved version of the Bergmann pistol No. 3 had been developed in 1896, being released for sale in the same year as M 96. The No. 3 M 96 cartridge was most widely used in the Bergmann pistols manufactured at Gaggenau. The same cartridge was later produced in many European ammunition plants and was commercially available until about 1930.

Bullet diameter	6·65 – 6·92 mm
Case length	21·60 – 22·00 mm
Case material	brass
Propellant	smokeless
Priming	Berdan
Round length	29·95 – 30·95 mm
Muzzle velocity	215 m/sec
Muzzle energy	93 J
Length of test barrel	108 mm

5. 7 mm Nambu

Cartridge for a smaller version of the 8 mm Nambu pistol adopted by the Imperial Japanese Army. According to some data this smaller-calibre pistol was reportedly issued to officers; other sources state that this pistol, introduced in 1929, was intended for civilian use only. The output of this cartridge was limited to Japan and was discontinued after the end of the war in 1945.

Bullet diameter	7·05 – 7·10 mm
Case length	19·55 – 19·80 mm
Case material	brass
Propellant	smokeless
Priming	Berdan
Round length	26·94 – 27·00 mm
Muzzle velocity	320 m/sec
Muzzle energy	184 J
Length of test barrel	83 mm

6. 7·25 mm Adler

This cartridge was evolved for the self-loading pistol produced in 1904 by the Adler-Waffenwerken (Engelbrecht & Wolff). Neither the pistol or the cartridge were widely used.

This cartridge can be easily mistaken for the 7 mm Charola cartridge and can only be distinguished by an exact measurement of the case: that of the Adler cartridge is slightly shorter and has a differently-formed neck.

Bullet diameter	7·07 – 7·15 mm
Case length	17·65 mm
Case material	brass
Propellant	smokeless
Priming	Berdan or Boxer

(no other
data available)

7. 7·5 mm Nagant

Cartridge for the Nagant revolver which was adopted by the Norwegian and Swedish Armies between 1887 and 1907. This revolver, developed by the Belgian Emile Nagant, was similar to the model adopted by the Tsarist Russian Army. Normally, the cartridge contained a paper-patched lead bullet but was also manufactured by some firms with a lead bullet without the paper patch, i.e. offered with a solid jacket bullet. Until quite recently, this cartridge was produced by NORMA with a differently-shaped lead bullet.

Bullet diameter	7·74 – 8·20 mm
Case length	22·10 – 23·10 mm
Case material	brass
Propellant	gunpowder; smokeless
Priming	Berdan
Round length	31·92 – 34·93 mm
Muzzle velocity	225 m/sec
Muzzle energy	176 J
Length of test barrel	110 mm

8. 7·5 mm Swiss Ordnance

Cartridge for the Swiss Army revolver used between 1882 and 1903. This sidearm was based on the Chamelot-Delvigne system and improved by Col R. Schmidt. It remained in service with some units even after the official adoption of the Luger pistol.

The initial cartridges had paper-patched lead bullets replaced by a solid jacket bullet, while the civil (commercial) version was produced without the paper patch. This cartridge was manufactured in differing variants by several European ammunition firms until 1935. It is interchangeable with the 7·5 mm Nagant cartridge and can only be distinguished by its headstamp.

Bullet diameter	7·75 – 8·30 mm
Case length	22·30 – 22·85 mm
Case material	brass
Propellant	gunpowder
Priming	Berdan
Round length	33·94 – 35·50 mm
Muzzle velocity	221 m/sec
Muzzle energy	176 J
Length of test barrel	114 mm

9. 7·62 mm Nagant

This cartridge was evolved for the gas-seal revolver adopted by the Tsarist Russian Army in 1895. The bullet is completely enclosed in the case and is set slightly deeper than the top rim of it. The gas seal is achieved by the case protruding 1·7 mm ahead of the cylinder which is pushed forward exactly that distance when cocking the revolver. This is also the reason for the typically long striker on the hammer. The effect of this technical refinement is a notably higher effective gas pressure and therefore higher muzzle velocity.

The Nagant revolver and its cartridge found a widespread use in Europe. A sports revolver of this type and calibre plays an important role even today, except that its cartridges would be loaded with woodcutter bullets.

Bullet diameter	7·79 – 7·82 mm
Case length	38·35 – 38·75 mm
Case material	brass
Propellant	gunpowder; smokeless
Priming	Berdan
Round length	38·35 – 38·75 mm
Muzzle velocity	290 m/sec
Muzzle energy	285 J
Length of test barrel	110 mm

10. 7·62 mm Tokarev

As far as its performance is concerned this cartridge is generally similar to the 7·63 Mauser. It was evolved by Fyodor V. Tokarev for the self-loading pistol of his design which was adopted by the Red Army in 1930.

Later on, the 7·62 mm Tokarev cartridge was replaced in the Soviet Army by the 9 mm Makarov, but it is still in use in the Czechoslovak Army for their M-52 military pistol and various sub-machine guns. (The 7·62 mm Tokarev cartridge was used by all Soviet sub-machine guns throughout the war years, and for a period afterwards, and was produced in many millions. In 1944 the standard equipment of most Soviet assault section of 10-12 men included 5-6 sub-machine guns, the highest infantry fire-power of any army at the time. The 9 mm Makarov pistol did not appear until 1952. *Tr*)

Bullet diameter	7·78 – 7·82 mm
Case length	24·45 – 24·80 mm
Case material	brass, steel
Propellant	smokeless
Priming	Berdan
Round length	34·69 – 34·80 mm
Muzzle velocity	455 m/sec
Muzzle energy	569 J
Length of test barrel	116 mm

11. 7·63 mm Mauser

This cartridge is of similar dimensions to the 7·65 mm Mannlicher and 7·65 mm Mannlicher and 7·65 mm Borchardt cartridges but carries a more powerful propellant charge and therefore cannot be fired from the Borchardt or Mannlicher pistols Model 1896.

It was specially evolved for the Mauser pistol Model 1896 (C/96), is closely identical to the 7·62 mm Tokarev cartridge and, on account of its almost identical performance, is also interchangeable with it.

The 7·63 mm Mauser cartridge found a world-wide use in various pistols, although the Mauser pistol intended for it was never officially adopted as a sidearm by any army.

(In its day, the top-loading Mauser C/96 with its wooden holster was one of the most popular sidearms due to its 10-round magazine capacity, hitting power and long range. It was a favourite weapon of the 1905 revolutionaries in Russia, the Red Army cavalry and, later, the Chinese Army. Closer home, it was also Winston Churchill's trusted gun in South Africa during the Boer War. The pistol is known as the 'Broomhandle'. *Tr*)

Bullet diameter	7·67 – 7·85 mm
Case length	24·00 – 25·50 mm
Case material	brass, lacquered steel
Propellant	smokeless
Priming	Berdan or Boxer
Round length	–
Muzzle velocity	443 m/sec
Muzzle energy	539 J
Length of test barrel	140 mm

12. 7·63 mm Mannlicher

The Mannlicher self-loading pistol Model 1901 was offered as a military sidearm to the Austro-Hungarian Army by its designer, Ferdinand Ritter von Mannlicher, but was not accepted. However, after its adoption by several South American states the pistol and its cartridge found a more widespread application.

The 7·63 mm Mannlicher cartridge was produced in various European ammunition factories until the late 1930s and is reportedly still being manufactured in Argentina.

Bullet diameter	7·65 – 7·82 mm
Case length	20·80 – 21·00 mm
Case material	brass
Propellant	smokeless
Priming	Berdan
Round length	28·15 – 28·70 mm
Muzzle velocity	312 m/sec
Muzzle energy	267 J
Length of test barrel	160 mm

13. 7·65 mm Borchardt

The Borchardt self-loading pistol found only limited use in its time, but is now highly regarded in the specialist literature owing to its trend-setting design.

The 7·65 mm Borchardt cartridge hardly differs from the 7·63 mm Mauser, and can only be distinguished by the inscription on its cartridge box. This cartridge cannot be said to have had any significant influence on the development of other, longer-used cartridges, such as the Mauser, Mannlicher or Tokarev.

Bullet diameter	7·79 – 7·80 mm
Case length	25·10 – 25·20 mm
Case material	brass
Propellant	smokeless
Priming	Berdan
Round length	34·10 mm
Muzzle velocity	385 m/sec
Muzzle energy	407 J
Length of test barrel	190 mm

14. 7·62 mm Browning

Evolved in 1897 by John M. Browning and introduced commercially by the FN concern at Herstal in Belgium for their Model 1900 self-loading pistol. A few years later the cartridge was adopted by Colt at Hartford, Conn., USA, under the designation ·32 Automatic (·32 ACP) for their larger pocket pistols.

Numerous self-loading pistols were developed to use the 7·65 mm Browning cartridge, of which the Walther pistols are the

All captioned from left to right:

5 mm Bergmann No. 2 M 96, 6·35 mm Browning, 7·62 mm Nagant, 7·62 mm Tokarev

7·63 mm Mauser, 7·63 mm Mannlicher, 7·65 mm Long, 7·65 mm Browning

8 mm Dormus, 6·5 mm Bergmann No. 3 M 96, 6·5 mm Bergmann No. 3 M 96

7·5 mm Nagant, 7·5 mm Swiss Ordnance, 7·5 mm Gysi, 7·5 mm Swiss Ordnance (early mfg).

7·65 mm Parabellum (Finnish mfg), 7·65 mm Parabellum (Swiss mfg), 8 mm Lebel, 8 mm Gasser

7·65 mm Frommer, 7 mm Bergmann-Simplex, 9 mm Bergmann No. 6

229

best known in Germany. It is still widely used for self-defence weapons, despite the trend towards more powerful cartridges. Even a sub-machine gun of this calibre is still available. However, the 7·65 mm cartridge has lost its once-leading position in the German police armament.

Bullet diameter	7·70 – 7·95 mm
Case length	16·90 – 17·28 mm
Case material	brass, metal
Propellant	smokeless
Priming	Berdan or Boxer
Round length	24·60 – 25·00 mm
Muzzle velocity	300 m/sec
Muzzle energy	212 J
Length of test barrel	90 mm

15. 7·65 mm Parabellum

Cartridge for the self-loading pistol evolved by Georg Luger and patented in 1900. This pistol was a redesign of the 1893 Borchardt pistol which was rather unwieldly for practical use. The new handgun was adopted by the Swiss Army as the Luger Pistol in 1903.

The early cartridges of this type had truncated cone-shaped bullets, replaced later by round-headed bullets.

The Luger pistol came into widespread use, as did its cartridge, which is still being produced by several ammunition factories at present.

Bullet diameter	7·70 – 7·90 mm
Case length	21·32 – 21·60 mm
Case material	brass, aluminium
Propellant	smokeless
Priming	Berdan or Boxer
Round length	23·70 – 30·15 mm
Muzzle velocity	368 m/sec
Muzzle energy	406 J
Length of test barrel	120 mm

16. 7·65 mm Frommer

Cartridge for the self-loading pistol designed by Rudolf Frommer, which became known as the Frommer Model 1901.

This cartridge is identical to the 7·65 mm Roth-Sauer, but features a more powerful propellant charge. The Frommer cartridge can only be distinguished by its headstamp: F-CY/F/P/BP. Both the Frommer pistol and its cartridge were manufactured until the beginning of the First World War.

Bullet diameter	7·72 – 7·80 mm
Case length	12·95 – 13·10 mm
Case material	brass
Propellant	smokeless
Priming	Berdan
Round length	21·42 – 21·44 mm
Muzzle velocity	340 m/sec
Muzzle energy	266 J
Length of test barrel	100 mm

17. ·32 Browning Automatic (·32 ACP)

This semi-rimmed cartridge was evolved in 1907 and intended for a semi-automatic Colt pistol; it can be regarded as variant of the 7·65 mm Browning (·32 ACP) cartridge.

The case has an annular lead strip inside its neck, similar to the ·35 cartridge used by the Smith & Wesson pistol.

Bullet diameter	7·80 (at cartridge mouth); 8·00 – 8·03 mm
Case length	16·97 – 17·12 mm
Case material	brass
Propellant	smokeless
Priming	gunpowder
Round length	24·97 – 25·07 mm
Muzzle velocity	–
Muzzle energy	–
Length of test barrel	–

18. 7·65 mm Longue

Cartridge for the MAS self-loading pistol adopted by the French Army as Model 1935A. The development of this cartridge goes back to the 1925; from 1935 until the end of the Second World War it was manufactured by various State-owned and private French ammunition factories.

Bullet diameter	7·80 – 7·90 mm
Case length	19·50 – 19·70 mm
Case material	brass, steel, lacquered steel
Propellant	smokeless
Priming	Berdan
Round length	30·20 – 30·35 mm
Muzzle velocity	358 m/sec
Muzzle energy	363 J
Length of test barrel	105 mm

19. 7·7 mm Bittner

Cartridge for the repeating pistol designed in 1893 by Gustav Bittner at Weipert in Bohemia. Neither the weapon or its cartridge found widespread application, so that both should now be considered among the most desirable rarities from the collector's point of view.

The cartridge was produced in limited numbers by the RWS (Rheinisch-Westfälische Sprengstoff Aktiengesellschaft) at Nürnberg.

Bullet diameter	7·68 – 7·70 mm
Case length	16·80 – 16·90 mm
Case material	brass
Propellant	smokeless
Priming	Berdan
Round length	26·50 – 26·52 mm
Muzzle velocity	–
Muzzle energy	–
Length of test barrel	–

20. 8 mm Dormus

No details regarding the shape and ballistic data of this cartridge have appeared in the literature to date. All that can be said is that it had a cylindrical, rimless case, as indicated by the cartridge chamber of the sole example of this weapon available for examination.

This cartridge was made for the self-loading pistol designed in 1894 by Georg Ritter von Dormus according to plans prepared by Karl Salvator, the Archduke of Austria and Field-marshal of the Imperial Austro-Hungarian Army. The handgun itself became known as the Dormus pistol.

(No data available)

21. 8 mm Schlegelmilch

To date hardly any useful information about this cartridge has come to light. Neither the pistol it was evolved for, nor the cartridge, reached series-production and consequently both had only a limited application. The weapon itself was a self-loading pistol designed by Louis Schlegelmilch, a foreman at the Königliche Waffen- und Munitionsfabrik (Royal Arms and Ammunition Factory), Spandau. This handgun is better known as the Spandau self-loading pistol M 1896.

(No data available)

22. 8 mm Bergmamm-Simplex

This cartridge was evolved in 1897 for the Simplex self-loading pistol, which was designed by Theodor Bergmann at Gaggenau in Baden and manufactured according to his patent in Belgium under the above designation. The cartridge was produced by various European manufacturers and was commercially available until the 1930s.

Bullet diameter	7·98 – 8·03 mm
Case length	17·80 – 18·20 mm
Case material	brass
Propellant	smokeless
Priming	Berdan
Round length	24·50 – 25·00 mm
Muzzle velocity	240 m/sec
Muzzle energy	137 J
Length of test barrel	68 mm

23. 8 mm Bergmann No. 4 (and No. 7)

This is the third and largest calibre in the range of Bergmann pistols (5 mm, 6·6 mm and 8 mm). The Model No. 4 was an improvement of the first design by Louis Schmeisser of 1894. The cartridge case had an ejector rim, and was produced by various ammunition factories until about 1910. However, neither the weapon or its cartridge were widely used.

The cartridge No. 7 is very similar and has almost identical data, although its case is 2 mm shorter. Both the handgun and its cartridge found only limited application.

Bullet diameter	8·00 − 8·05 mm
Case length	21·80 − 22·20 mm
Case material	brass
Propellant	smokeless
Priming	Berdan
Round length	30·25 − 30·65 mm
Muzzle velocity	−
Muzzle energy	−
Length of test barrel	−

24. 8 mm Lebel

Cartridge for the French revolver Model 1886, generally known as the Lebel revolver. The concept of this handgun was worked out by a commission chaired by Col. Nicolas Lebel. This rather small-calibre cartridge for those days was adopted as early as 1886, while the revolver belonging to it was not accepted until 1892, one year after the death of Col. Lebel.

Originally, the cartridge had a lead bullet, replaced later by a copper-jacketed one. This cartridge was produced in various European ammunition factories and was available until the end of the Second World War.

Bullet diameter	8·00 − 8·40 mm
Case length	26·10 − 27·60 mm
Case material	brass
Propellant	smokeless
Priming	Berdan
Round length	36·10 − 36·96 mm
Muzzle velocity	260 m/sec

Muzzle energy	245 J
Length of test barrel	116 mm

25. 8 mm Gasser

This cartridge was originally evolved for the Austrian Rast & Gasser revolver Model 1898, but a number of revolvers for this cartridge were later also designed in other countries.

The Army-type cartridge had a flat-nosed bullet with a hard-lead core, produced by G. Roth in Vienna and Sellier & Bellot in Prague, but similar cartridges were also manufactured in other European ammunition factories. It is still on the production programme of the Italian firm of Fiocchi, which has firm orders for it.

Bullet diameter	7·92 − 8·25 mm
Case length	26·35 − 27·50 mm
Case material	brass
Propellant	smokeless
Priming	Berdan
Round length	36·35 − 36·60 mm
Muzzle velocity	240 m/sec
Muzzle energy	322 J
Length of test barrel	116 mm

26. 8 mm Nambu

This cartridge was manufactured exclusively in Japan until the end of the Second World War for the similarly-named self-loading pistol designed by Col. K. Nambu, which was adopted by the Imperial Japanese Army in 1914.

Numerous alterations were incorporated into this handgun during its production life, but the cartridge remained unchanged.

Postwar, this cartridge was manufactured in the USA by the B & E Cartridge Company in Minneapolis for gun collectors and other interested parties. The American-made version differs from the original Japanese cartridges by having a copper-jacketed bullet and a machine-turned case.

Bullet diameter	8·10 – 8·18 mm
Case length	21·20 – 21·85 mm
Case material	brass
Propellant	smokeless
Priming	Berdan
Round length	–
Muzzle velocity	325 m/sec
Muzzle energy	343 J
Length of test barrel	116 mm

27. 8 mm Roth-Steyr

Cartridge for the self-loading pistol adopted by the Austro-Hungarian Army in 1907. The Roth-Steyr pistol, the design of which was based on numerous experiments carried out by Karel Krnka, was produced in very large numbers by the Waffenfabriken Steyr (Steyr Arms Factories) in Austria.

The cartridge remained in production in several European countries until 1940 and is still being manufactured by the Italian firm of Fiocchi.

Bullet diameter	8·05 – 8·20 mm
Case length	18·50 – 18·80 mm
Case material	brass
Propellant	smokeless
Priming	Berdan
Round length	28·60 – 28·82 mm
Muzzle velocity	320 m/sec
Muzzle energy	382 J
Length of test barrel	125 mm

28. 8 mm Steyr

This cartridge was evolved as an experimental round for the revolver designed by the Steyr arms factory.

Neither the handgun nor the cartridge reached the series-production stage. The case of this cartridge was also used for the 8 mm Kromar pistol cartridge.

Bullet diameter	8·00 – 8·20 mm
Case length	22·53 – 22·65 mm
Case material	brass

Propellant	smokeless
Priming	Berdan
Round length	32·75 mm
Muzzle velocity	–
Muzzle energy	–
Length of test barrel	–

29. 8·5 mm Mars

This is the smallest calibre in the Mars pistol range; the others were all 9 mm and 10 mm.

The cartridge was evolved in about 1910 by H.W. Gabbett-Fairfax in England and intended for a self-loading pistol of his own design. Although the handgun was tested by a British examination commission, it was finally turned down as unsuitable for military service. Neither the weapon or its cartridge reached the series-production stage.

Bullet diameter	8·50 mm
Case length	26·00 mm
Case material	brass
Propellant	smokeless; cordite
Priming	Berdan
Round length	36·60 – 36·62 mm
Muzzle velocity	535 m/sec
Muzzle energy	1288 J
Length of test barrel	229 mm

30. 9 mm French Rand (9 mm Galand revolver)

This so-called thick-rimmed 9 mm cartridge is the medium calibre of the series comprising the 7 mm, 9 mm and 12 mm cartridges. It was evolved for revolvers which had been modified according to the Lefaucheaux system from pin-fire to centre-fire priming. This cartridge found very widespread use in Europe and was commercially available until about 1914.

Bullet diameter	9·08 – 9·55 mm
Case length	13·00 – 14·50 mm
Case material	brass
Propellant	gunpowder
Priming	inside primed, battery cup, Boxer

8 mm Steyr, 8 mm Nambu, 9 mm Parabellum (Swiss mfg),
9 mm Browning Short.

9 mm Steyr, 9 mm Bergmann-Bayard (9 mm Largo), 9 mm
Glisenti, 9 mm Long.

7·65 mm Browning (·32 ACP), 9 mm Browning Short (·380
ACP), ·380 Revolver MK II, ·44 Smith & Wesson Russian.

9 mm Makarov, ·38 Automatic, 9 mm Danish Army, 10·6
mm German Ordnance.

A selection of 9 mm Parabellum cartridges incl. training
and blank rounds.

Round length	22·50 – 25·77 mm
Muzzle velocity	–
Muzzle energy	–
Length of test barrel	–

31. 9 mm Danish Army

Cartridge for the Danish Army revolver Model 91 which was still used by various (Danish) units during the Second World War.

This cartridge was manufactured exclusively by the Danish State ammunition factory Haerens Ammunitionsarsenalet, although in about 1900 production was also undertaken by the DWM in Germany.

Bullet diameter	9·40 – 9·65 mm
Case length	16·90 – 17·58 mm
Case material	brass
Propellant	smokeless
Priming	Berdan
Round length	27·28 – 27·32 mm
Muzzle velocity	200 m/sec
Muzzle energy	160 J
Length of test barrel	–

32. 9 mm Campo Giro

Details of this cartridge are contradictory in specialist literature. According to Erlmeier-Brandt, the few available data indicate a strong similarity with the 9 mm Bergmann-Bayard and Bergmann No. 6. However, it it not clear whether the 9 mm Campo Giro was identical to the 9 mm Bergmann No. 6 to begin with, or the Campo Giro pistol was adapted for the 9 mm Bergmann No. 6 cartridge.

Bullet diameter	–	
Case length	–	
Case material	brass	
Propellant	smokeless	(no other
Priming	Berdan	details
Round length	32·00 mm	available)
Muzzle velocity	270 m/sec	
Muzzle energy	–	
Length of test barrel	–	

33. 9 mm Bergmann-Bayard (9 mm Largo)

The 9 mm Bergmann-Bayard and the No. 6 cartridges are almost alike, and can only be told apart by their slightly different length (due to the different setting of the bullets). The 9 mm Bergmann-Bayard was manufactured in several European ammunition factories, and is still being produced in Spain under the designation 9 mm Largo.

This cartridge can also be mistaken for the 9 mm Steyr which however has a bullet of different weight. The 9 mm Bergmann-Bayard was used in the self-loading pistol No. 6 Model 1903 which was adopted by the Danish Army in 1910.

Bullet diameter	9·05 – 9·10 mm
Case length	22·80 – 23·00 mm
Case material	brass
Propellant	smokeless
Priming	Berdan
Round length	32·90 – 33·80 mm
Muzzle velocity	340 m/sec
Muzzle energy	509 J
Length of test barrel	102 mm

34. 9 mm Parabellum

This cartridge was evolved in 1902 by the DWM for the self-loading military pistol designed by Georg Luger, originally of 7·65 mm calibre. The 9 mm cartridge, together with the Navy model of the Parabellum pistol were adopted in Germany in 1904, although the standard-size Parabellum pistol was not accepted for military service until 1908.

Even today, the 9 mm Parabellum is still a highly topical cartridge for powerful self-loading pistols, sports pistols and revolvers. More so in fact, because over the last few years the standard side arms of the German police are also gradually changing over to this cartridge.

Due to its popularity there is a corresponding multitude of modifications regarding the shape and weight of the bullet, as well as various developments for special purposes (such as bullets with incendiary charges or a steel core). The 9 mm Parabellum also served as basis for the less powerful Italian 9 mm Glisenti which was manufactured exclusively in Italy for the Glisenti pistols and can easily be mistaken for the original German cartridge.

Bullet diameter	8·90 – 9·05 mm
Case length	18·80 – 19·20 mm
Case material	brass, lacquered steel, aluminium, copper-covered steel
Propellant	smokeless
Priming	Berdan or Boxer
Round length	28·90 – 29·85 mm
Muzzle velocity	345 m/sec
Muzzle energy	476 J
Length of test barrel	125 mm

35. 9 mm Browning Short (·380 ACP or ·380 Auto)

Since its introduction in 1908 this cartridge has been used in numerous self-defence and military pistols, and is still part of the manufacturing programme of most ammunition factories.

The 9 mm Browning Short was evolved by Colt in Hartford, Conn., USA, in 1908 and initially sold commercially under the designation ·380 ACP (Automatic Colt Pistol). A short while later the cartridge was adopted by the FN in Belgium for their self-loading pistol Model 1910.

Bullet diameter	8·85 – 9·05 mm
Case length	17·00 – 17·35 mm
Case material	brass
Propellant	smokeless
Priming	Berdan or Boxer
Round length	–
Muzzle velocity	270 m/sec
Muzzle energy	222 J
Length of test barrel	90 mm

36. 9 mm Glisenti

Externally this cartridge is completely identical to the 9 mm Parabellum (truncated-cone-bullet version), but is almost one third less powerful. This reduction was required for the 9 mm Glisenti self-loading pistol Model 1910, and for that reason the cartridge is not interchangeable with the 9 mm Parabellum.

The only certain identification is by means of the headstamp. The Glisenti cartridge was manufactured exclusively in Italy for the pistol of the same name adopted by the Italian Army. It was used officially until 1938, but the cartridge was still manufactured until quite recently for private customers by the Fiocchi company.

Bullet diameter	8·95 – 9·00 mm
Case length	18·90 – 19·00 mm
Case material	brass
Propellant	smokeless
Priming	Berdan
Round length	28·90 – 29·00 mm
Muzzle velocity	–
Muzzle energy	–
Length of test barrel	–

37. 9 mm Steyr

This cartridge can be easily mistaken for the 9 mm Bergmann-Bayard. The only certain way of identifying it is by checking the weight of the bullet, which is slightly less in the 9 mm Steyr.

The 9 mm Steyr was evolved in Austria for the Steyr self-loading pistol Model 1911, which was adopted by the Imp. Austro-Hungarian and Romanian Armies.

Bullet diameter	8·95 – 9·05 mm
Case length	22·70 – 23·20 mm
Case material	brass
Propellant	smokeless
Priming	Berdan
Round length	32·83 – 33·30 mm
Muzzle velocity	361 m/sec
Muzzle energy	495 J
Length of test barrel	127 mm

38. 9 mm Mauser Versuch III

The Versuch (Experimental) III cartridge is externally very similar to the 9 mm Parabellum, but carries a different headstamp: DWM KK 487C. It was developed by the DWM in co-operation with Mauser AG Oberndorf for the self-loading pistol Model 1912/14 delivered to Tsarist Russia and Brazil. Of the four Mauser experimental cartridges (I to IV) only III was manufactured in series for a relatively short time, its production terminating at the beginning of the First World War

Bullet diameter	9·00 – 9·10 mm
Case length	18·80 – 19·00 mm
Case material	brass
Propellant	smokeless
Priming	Berdan
Round length	29·50 – 29·70 mm
Muzzle velocity	–
Muzzle energy	–
Length of test barrel	–

39. 9 mm Browning Long

This cartridge was evolved by John M. Browning for the military pistol Model 1903 in the same year. Afterwards, it was used in numerous other self-loading pistols as well as some sub-machine guns. The 9 mm Browning Long was manufactured by most European ammunition factories, as well as by Remington in the USA. Its production ended in about 1950, with the exception of the Fiocchi company in Italy.

Bullet diameter	8·95 – 9·09 mm
Case length	20·00 – 20·30 mm
Case material	brass
Propellant	smokeless
Priming	Boxer or Berdan
Round length	27·45 – 28·00 mm
Muzzle velocity	335 m/sec
Muzzle energy	400 J
Length of test barrel	128 mm

40. 9 mm Makarov

Cartridge evolved and produced in the Soviet Union after the Second World War for the Makarov self-loading pistol, still the official side-arm of the Soviet and Soviet-bloc armed forces.

Its performance falls about half-way between those of the 9 mm Browning Short and the 9 mm Parabellum, and thus the 9 mm Makarov represents a close relative to the pre-war German 9 mm Ultra (9 mm Super) cartridge project. The Soviet Stetchkin pistol – which can also be used as a sub-machine gun – was also designed for this cartridge.

Bullet diameter	9·23 – 9·25 mm
Case length	17·85 – 18·05 mm
Case material	brass, copper-covered or lacquered steel
Propellant	smokeless
Priming	Berdan
Round length	24·80 – 24·95 mm
Muzzle velocity	340 m/sec
Muzzle energy	365 J
Length of test barrel	93 mm

41. 9·1 mm Abadie

This cartridge has very similar measurements to the 9 mm Danish Army cartrige and can only be definitely identified by its Portuguese headstamp. It was used in the Portuguese Army Abadie revolver Model 1878.

Bullet diameter	9·45 – 9·55 mm
Case length	17·45 – 17·52 mm
Case material	brass
Propellant	gunpowder
Priming	–
Round length	27·30 mm
Muzzle velocity	162 m/sec
Muzzle energy	127 J
Length of test barrel	–

42. ·380 Revolver Mk I

Replaced the ·380 CF revolver cartridge. It was first produced for the British Army in 1937 and differed from Mk II cartridges by having a lead bullet. It was officially adopted in service on 17 June 1937 as 'Cartridge Small Arms, Ball, Revolver, ·380 inch, Mk I'. The bullet weighs 13 g, is made of lead/zinc or lead/antimony alloy and propelled by 0·22 g of smokeless powder charge achieves a muzzle velocity of approx 180 m/sec.

Bullet diameter	9·00 – 9·15 mm
Case length	19·30 – 19·40 mm
Case material	brass
Propellant	smokeless
Priming	Berdan or Boxer
Round length	31·42 – 31·50 mm
Muzzle velocity	183 m/sec
Muzzle energy	221 J
Length of test barrel	102 mm

43. ·380 Revolver Mk II

Successor to Cartridge ·380, Revolver Mk I and has a copper/nickel-alloy-jacketed bullet weighing 11·5 g. This cartridge was adopted by the British Army on 22 October 1937.

The Mk II has a propellant charger of 0·26 g of cordite, while the 2z variant has 0·15 g of nitro-cellulose.

Bullet diameter	9·00 – 9·05 mm
Case length	19·25 – 19·45 mm
Case material	brass
Propellant	smokeless
Priming	Berdan or Boxer
Round length	30·55 – 31·50 mm
Muzzle velocity	–
Muzzle energy	–
Length of test barrel	–

44. ·38 Special

The ·38 Smith & Wesson Special has been one of the most popular revolver cartridges for some time. Owing to its accuracy it is readily used for target practice, particularly with the woodcutter bullet and reduced powder charge. In addition it is also a cartridge widely used for self-defence purposes and much used by the police, especially in the USA.

Its development goes back to 1899 when it was conceived as ammunition for the Revolver ·38 Hand Ejector Military & Police. This initial version had a longer case. Afterwards it was manufactured in many variants all over the world. In addition, there were privately produced reload versions. As a result, the muzzle velocity can range from 222 to 418 m/sec and the weight of the bullet vary from 7·5 to 13·0 grammes. The normal standard version has a bullet of about 10·2 grammes.

Bullet diameter	8·55 – 9·25 mm
Case length	28·19 – 29·67 mm
Case material	brass, nickelled brass
Propellant	gunpowder, minimum smoke, smokeless
Priming	Berdan or Boxer
Round length	35·00 – 40·00 mm
Muzzle velocity	222 – 418 m/sec
Muzzle energy	326 – 719 J
Length of test barrel	152 mm (6 in)

45. ·38 Automatic (·38 ACP)

In its dimensions and performance this cartridge largely corresponds to the ·38 Super Automatic. It was evolved and produced by the Colt company in the USA for their self-loading pistol Model 1900. Other pistols designed to use this cartridge were the Webley & Scott and some Astra and Star models in Spain.

Bullet diameter	8·97 – 9·13 mm
Case length	22·20 – 23·00 mm
Case material	brass
Propellant	smokeless
Priming	Berdan or Boxer
Round length	31·77 – 32·88 mm
Muzzle velocity	317 m/sec
Muzzle energy	430 J
Length of test barrel	114 mm

46. 10·4 mm Italian Ordnance

Originally belonged to the Chamelot-Delvigne revolver officially adopted by the Italian Army in 1874. The revolver was soon replaced by other models but the cartridge remained in use. It has been established that the 10·4 mm cartridges with lead bullets had longer cases than those loaded with jacketed bullets.

The production of this cartridge was limited to Italy where it terminated in about the mid-1930s.

Bullet diameter	10·52 – 11·05 mm
Case length	21·70 – 22·75 mm
Case material	brass
Propellant	gunpowder; smokeless
Priming	Berdan
Round length	31·65 – 32·25 mm; 29·68 – 29·82 mm
Muzzle velocity	255 m/sec
Muzzle energy	287 J
Length of test barrel	114 mm

47. 10·6 mm German Ordnance

This cartridge can be mistaken for the 10·6 mm Mauser evolved for the Mauser revolver Model 1878 (the so-called 'Zick-Zack Revolver'). It was not accepted by the military and found only limited use.

The 10·6 mm German Ordnance cartridge was developed for the Ordnance revolver adopted by the German Army in 1879, known as the 'Reichsrevolver'. The same ammunition was also used in the later Model 84 revolver. This 10·6 mm cartridge was manufactured only in Germany, and was in production until the end of the First World War.

Bullet diameter	10·75 – 11·00 mm
Case length	24·50 – 24·90 mm
Case material	brass
Propellant	gunpowder; Rifle Powder 71
Priming	Berdan
Round length	34·95 – 36·90 mm
Muzzle velocity	205 m/sec

Muzzle energy	347 J
Length of test barrel	180 mm

48. 11 mm Devillers

This is not a proper cartridge in the accepted sense of the word. It was evolved by Dr Devillers, chairman of a Paris pistol sport club in 1908 and instead of the usual lead bullet features one shaped from wax. These wax bullets were set right into the case, level with its mouth, or protruded about halfway outside.

This type of cartridge was used as ammunition for the 'mock duels' very popular at the time, where the duellers stood about 20 m apart and wore face masks similar to those used by fencers.

The Devillers cartridges were made in 11 mm, 8 mm Lebel and ·44 S & W Russian calibres, so that all the most popular revolvers then in use could fire this special ammunition. They were sold as ready-made or reload cartridges.

Bullet diameter	11·00 mm
Case length	24·45 – 24·50 mm
Case material	brass/steel
Propellant	none
Priming	special form
Round length	24·45 – 30·70 mm
Muzzle velocity	–
Muzzle energy	–
Length of test barrel	–

49. 11 mm French Ordnance

Cartridge for the French Chamelot-Delvigne revolver, adopted by the French Army in 1873. It was produced exclusively by French ammunition factories and remained commercially available until the mid-1930s.

Bullet diameter	11·35 – 11·75 mm
Case length	17·05 – 18·20 mm
Case material	brass
Propellant	gunpowder
Priming	battery cup, Berdan

Round length	29·00 – 30·20 mm
Muzzle velocity	245 m/sec
Muzzle energy	343 J
Length of test barrel	112 mm

50. 11·25 mm Norwegian

Cartridge for the Norwegian-built version of the Colt Automatic Pistol Model 1911 (later known as Colt Government Model) which was in service with various Norwegian formations. This cartridge is identical to the American ·45 ACP and interchangeable with it. An exact identification can be made only by checking the headstamp.

Bullet diameter	11·27 – 11·47 mm
Case length	22·72 – 22·95 mm
Case material	brass
Propellant	smokeless
Priming	Boxer
Round length	32·02 – 32·15 mm
Muzzle velocity	(other data as ·45 ACP)
Muzzle energy	
Length of test barrel	

51. 11·35 mm Schouboe

This cartridge was evolved by I.T. Schouboe, Chief Engineer of the Dansk Rekylriffel Syndikat (DRS) in cooperation with the DWM in Germany, and was intended for the Schouboe self-loading pistol which had gone into series production in 1904. However, as this handgun never aroused any great interest its cartridge also frailed to find any other application and production was terminated in both DWM and DRS factories in the early 1920s.

Bullet diameter	11·25 – 11·47 mm
Case length	17·70 – 18·20 mm
Case material	brass
Propellant	smokeless
Priming	Berdan
Round length	28·60 – 29·25 mm
Muzzle velocity	495 m/sec
Muzzle energy	453 J
Length of test barrel	124 mm

52. 11·5 mm Werder

This cartridge was evolved in 1869 and could be fired from the Werder carbine and the Werder pistol, but not from the Werder rifle. The cases of these cartridges manufactured in State arsenals feature a pressed base while those made elsewhere have the so-called Mauser base.

The Werder carbines were produced in Germany until about 1910. The round is also known as the 11·5 mm German target (practice) cartridge.

Bullet diameter	11·35 – 11·85 mm
Case length	34·80 – 35·40 mm
Case material	brass
Propellant	gunpowder
Priming	Berdan
Round length	49·40 – 50·25 mm
Muzzle velocity	–
Muzzle energy	–
Length of test barrel	–

53 ·44 Smith & Wesson Russian

The development of this cartridge began with a Russian order for a new military revolver to Smith and Wesson in 1871. In the course of years this revolver was continually modified, so that in the end it also required a considerably changed cartridge.

Compared to the ·44 Smith & Wesson American the weight of the bullet was increased by 1·8 grammes while the powder charge was reduced by 0·3 g. The result was an increase in the muzzle velocity of about 30 m/sec.

Due to its accuracy and ease of reloading this cartridge was very popular with the sports shooting fraternity in its day. It was produced in numerous variations, with loads ranging from ordinary lead bullets to round bullets fitted deep in the case. Another change during its progressive development concerned the lubrication of the bullet. Initially it was lubricated externally, then internally, and finally evolved as a self-lubricating bullet – a lubricant carried inside the bullet is pressed against the barrel walls during the firing process.

The standard bullet weighs 16 g and is propelled by a 0.32 g of Dupont Pistol Powder No. 5, giving it a muzzle velocity of 235 m/sec. Cartridges manufactured by the RWS have a bullet weight of 15·9 g and a smokeless powder charge of 0.38 g, giving it a muzzle velocity of 232 m/sec.

Bullet diameter	19·50 – 21·23 mm
Case length	23·10 – 24·92 mm
Case material	brass, steel
Propellant	gunpowder, minimal smoke, smokeless
Priming	Berdan, Boxer, battery cup
Round length	34·40 – 37·00 mm
Muzzle velocity	235 m/sec
Muzzle energy	448 J
Length of test barrel	152 mm (6 in)

54. ·442 Webley
·442 Tranter/·442 British Tranter

This is a cartridge evolved specially for use in revolvers produced by the British firms of Enfield, Webley and Tranter. The Royal Irish Constabulary was armed with a Webley revolver of this calibre in about 1868.

The cartridge found widespread use in Europe, and was also produced in the USA under the designation ·44 Webley from about 1873 to 1939.

Bullet diameter	10·83 – 11·35 mm
Case length	16·41 – 17·50 mm
Case material	brass
Propellant	gunpowder, smokeless
Priming	Berdan, Boxer, battery cup
Round length	27·30 – 30·28 mm
Muzzle velocity	213 m/sec
Muzzle energy	330 J
Length of test barrel	102 mm

55. ·45 ACP (Automatic Colt Pistol)

This cartridge was evolved by John M.

Browning for his self-loading pistol as early as 1905; six years later the cartridge and the handgun were officially adopted by the US Army.

The reason for selecting such a large calibre stemmed directly from the evaluation of the unsatisfactory results achieved with the ·38 Long Colt cartridge during the Philippines campaign. The ·45 calibre was proposed by the Thompson-LaGarde Commission, with recommendation on no account to go below that. In addition to the Colt self-loading pistol already in service Smith & Wesson also produced a revolver for this cartridge in 1917. In this case, the cartridges were loaded with so-called 'Half-moon clips' which facilitated an easy loading and ejection of the rimless cartridge cases. This was followed in 1920 by the ·45 Auto Rim cartridge which did not need clips for loading.

The official designation of the above round was 'Cartridge, Ball, Caliber ·45, M1911'. It had a jacketed bullet weighing 15 g and a muzzle velocity of about 260 m/sec. It found a very widespread application in the Western world and is still part of the production programme of almost all ammunition factories.

The same cartridge is also in use in Norway for the military pistol M1914 where it is known as the 11·25 Norwegian.

Bullet diameter	11·12 – 11·45 mm
Case length	22·45 – 23·01 mm
Case material	brass, nickelled brass, lacquered steel, copper-covered steel, lead-covered steel, zink-covered steel, phosphated, aluminium
Propellant	smokeless
Priming	Berdan or Boxer
Round length	29·00 – 32·50 mm
Muzzle velocity	216 – 323 m/sec
Muzzle energy	325 – 1027 J
Length of test barrel	127 mm

56. ·455 Webley Mark I

It was officially adopted as 'Cartridge, Small

Arm, Ball, Pistol, Webley, Mark I, also Enfield' on 29 July 1891.(In English terminology the designation 'pistol' could stand for either that or a revolver.)

The 17 g bullet consists of a lead/zinc alloy in the proportion of 12:1. The cartridge has a 1·2 g black-powder-charge-type 'Rifled Pistol Powder' which gave the bullet a muzzle velocity of approx. 183 m/sec. This version was declared obsolete on 14 September 1894 and replaced by another cartridge which carried a charge of 0·42 g of cordite. The bullet remained the same. This cartridge was officially kept until 1921 when it was declared obsolete but not withdrawn from use until 19 March 1946.

Bullet diameter	11·45 – 11·57 mm
Case length	21·60 – 22·10 mm
Case material	brass
Propellant	gunpowder/smokeless
Priming	Boxer
Round length	36·30 – 36·78 mm
Muzzle velocity	216 m/sec
Muzzle energy	408 Joule
Length of test barrel	152 mm

57. ·455 Webley Mark II

After good experiences with the new cordite propellant, it was also used in this cartridge which was officially adopted on 21 July 1887 as 'Cartridge, Small Arm, Ball, Pistol, Webley, Cordite, Mark II'.

The new propellant allowed a shortening of the cartridge case by almost 3 mm. This cartridge was declared obsolete in 1898, only to be officially re-introduced on 14 July 1900. After the adoption of the Mark IV in 1909 the Mark II was again declared obsolete – only to be re-introduced for the third time in 1914, to be left in service until 1939.

The headstamp with the letter 'c' indicates cordite which ranged from 0·48 g in the early cartridges reducing to 0·45 g from about 1900 onwards. The bullet weight remained constant at 17 g.

Bullet diameter	11·52 – 11·57 mm

Case length	18·80 – 19·30 mm
Case material	brass
Propellant	smokeless
Priming	Berdan
Round length	31·52 – 31·92 mm
Muzzle velocity	183 m/sec
Muzzle energy	293 Joule
Length of test barrel	152 mm

58. ·455 Webley Mark III (and Mark IV)

The adoption by the British Army of the Mark II cartridge on 5 February 1898 soon proved to be an error that had to be quickly revised. The flattened nose bullet patented by Thomas W. Webley (GB Patent No 14754) was intended to have more stopping power but it infringed the Hague Declaration and rules on land warfare which forebade the use of bullets that had an excessive damaging effect. As a result, the Mark III cartridges were used up by the British Army in practice shoots.

The Mark IV cartridge with the modified bullet which was not so flat did not fare much better; it too was declared as unsuitable and the stocks used up as practice ammunition.

Bullet diameter	11·52 – 11·57 mm
Case length	18·80 – 19·30 mm
Case material	brass
Propellant	smokeless
Priming	Berdan
Round length	27·20 – 27·22 mm
Muzzle velocity	183 m/sec
Muzzle energy	242 J
Length of test barrel	152 mm

59. ·455 Webley Mark VI

Officially adopted for the British Army revolver on 18 September 1939, followed by its acceptance by the Royal Navy on 3 November 1939 and the RAF on 1 December 1939.

Basically, the Mark VI is nothing more than a variation of the Mark III which, with its flattened lead bullet, did not comply with the Hague rules for land warfare. On the Mark VI it was

Various versions of the ·38 Special

9 mm French Rand (9 mm Galand), 12 mm French Rand
(12 mm Galand)

Box of 11 mm Devillers cartridges for firing from
Galand revolvers

11·35 mm Schouboe, 11·5 mm Werder

11 mm French Ordnance, 11·25 mm Norwegian
(as ·45 ACP)

·442 Eley (·442 Webley), ·45 ACP, ·455 Webley Mk II,
·455 Webley Automatic Mk I, ·476 Enfield Mk III

replaced by a jacketed bullet. Loaded with
0·48 g of cordite, the 17 g bullet had a muzzle
velocity of approx. 190 m/sec. The designation
Mark VIz indicated cartridges loaded with
0·33 g of nitro-cellulose; they were also
distinguished by an additional 'z' on the
cartridge base.

The Mark VI cartridge was declared obsolete
for all branches of the (British) armed forces in
1946.

Bullet diameter	11·52 – 11·57 mm
Case length	18·80 – 19·30 mm
Case material	brass
Propellant	smokeless
Priming	Berdan
Round length	31·18 – 31·72 mm
Muzzle velocity	198 m/sec
Muzzle energy	343 J
Length of test barrel	152 mm

60. ·455 Webley Automatic Mk I

This represents the final stage of the British
pistol cartridges of this calibre. It was accepted
in 1912 for use in the Webley-Scott pistols in
service with the Royal Navy, and in 1915 for the
land forces of the RFC, followed in 1919 by the
RAF. In addition, from 1918 onwards Colt
pistols too were converted for this cartridge. In

1927 it was given the designation of Mk I.

The cartridge was withdrawn from service
use in 1938.

Bullet diameter	11·48 – 11·56 mm
Case length	23·06 – 23·62 mm
Case material	brass
Propellant	smokeless
Priming	Berdan
Round length	31·7 – 31·10 mm
Muzzle velocity	225 m/sec
Muzzle energy	375 J
Length of test barrel	127 mm

61. ·476 Enfield Mk III

This is the third version of the so-called Enfield
cartridges of which three different models are
known. It was introduced in (British) service on
10 December 1881 and known as '·476 Calibre',
which indicated the maximum diameter of the
bullet. A special feature of this bullet is the
deep hollow-out of its base which is closed by
a clay plug soaked in beeswax.

This cartridge was officially declared
obsolete on 26 September 1892 following the
adoption of the Webley Mk I (1891) cartridge.

Bullet diameter	12·04 – 12·12 mm
Case length	21·60 – 22·45 mm
Case material	brass
Propellant	gunpowder
Priming	Boxer
Round length	37·64 – 37·85 mm
Muzzle velocity	220 m/sec
Muzzle energy	435 J
Length of test barrel	152 mm (6 in)

62. 12 mm French Rand (12 mm Galand)

This is the largest calibre of the thick-rimmed
cartridges mentioned earlier. It was evolved
for those revolvers that had been converted
from pin-fire to centre-fire priming.

In the USA, this cartridge is better known as
the 12 mm Perrin, named after the supplier of

these revolvers at that time, L. Perrin & Cie of Paris.

Bullet diameter	11·00 – 11·80 mm
Case length	14·42 – 16·90 mm
Case material	brass, copper, steel
Propellant	black powder
Priming	inside primed, battery cup, Berdan
Round length	25·25 – 28·56 mm
Muzzle velocity	–
Muzzle energy	–
Length of test barrel	–

Commemorative weapons

Weapons gain their value as collectables because, as objects no longer made, they vividly document the technical development of a past epoch. Their present financial value in an economically stable period is directly related to their age, rarity and condition. A P-38 pistol dating from the final stages of the last war, showing nasty traces of its use, would be valued quite differently from, say, a Borchardt pistol in mint condition reposing it its case complete with accessories. Such a sketchy evaluation of a collectable firearm is in a way quite 'natural' because it arises from a continuous sequence of progressive development.

Another kind of highly valued collectable item is represented by engraved weapons, each of which is unique – unless decorated with a works engraving that has been repeated on several weapons. In this case the item is evaluated according to the age of the weapon and the effort expended on its engraving, its extent and the use of precious metals and fine woods. Whether this is to everybody's taste is another matter.

Another species of collectable guns are the so-called 'commemorative weapons' or 'commemorative models' which however cannot be considered uncritically. Quite often it is a matter of a strictly limited edition which artificially boosts the value of each individual weapon even in the absence of any corresponding increase in its production costs. Not infrequently the manufacturers support this trend by means of 'costings' that are far removed from reality. Favourite occasions for the issue of such mementos are the anniversary dates of the firms or the year of introduction of the given model.

The Walther concern chose the '50th birthday' of their Model PP to issue a quite decently fashioned PP pistol fitted with finely carved butt plates and a gold-plated hammer and trigger. In addition, the pistol features a gold-inlaid engraving on the slide '50 Jahre Walther PP 1929-1979'.

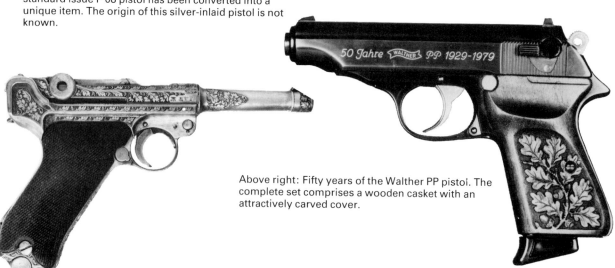

Above and below: By means of extensive engraving this standard issue P 08 pistol has been converted into a unique item. The origin of this silver-inlaid pistol is not known.

Above right: Fifty years of the Walther PP pistol. The complete set comprises a wooden casket with an attractively carved cover.

In the case of the Swiss SIG concern it was its 125th anniversary which led to the issue of a limited series of commemorative pistols in 1978. Packed in fitted mahogany cases and offered at a quite considerable price, according to the manufacturers all these handguns quickly found buyers.

A bigger series of anniversary weapons was issued by the Mauser concern in Germany over a period of years after 1970. These special models and certain typical postwar developments are shown on the following pages of this book. Each series was limited to 250 guns, and every pistol of this kind was distinguished by its extremely elegant finish, the effort expended on which serves as proof that such weapons could have hardly been sold with any real chance of commercial success in this age of mass-production. However, their retail price – and despite the undoubted quality of the product we have to mention this – does not really make it easy always to sell the complete series in the land of their origin, Germany. Such extremely beautiful models as the anniversary Mauser carbines, retailing at DM 8500, could after all only be made against firm orders, and most of them were reportedly sold abroad.

Above: On its 125th anniversary the SIG concern in Switzerland issued a limited series of handsomely adorned SIG-210 pistols.

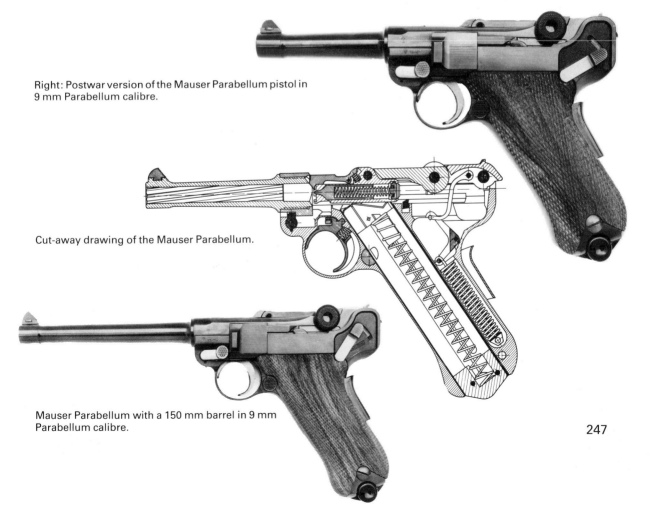

Right: Postwar version of the Mauser Parabellum pistol in 9 mm Parabellum calibre.

Cut-away drawing of the Mauser Parabellum.

Mauser Parabellum with a 150 mm barrel in 9 mm Parabellum calibre.

In technical concept these commemorative models are identical to the postwar versions of the 06/76 which correspond to the Model 29/70.

There was an interesting attempt to produce a sports version of the undoubtedly already very accurate Parabellum pistol by fitting it with appropriate sights and suitably modified trigger. This pistol was manufactured in 9 mm Parabellum calibre with a thick, rounded barrel and 7·65 mm Parabellum calibre with a laterally flattened barrel, necessary because of the breech function.

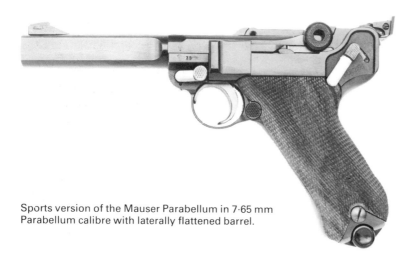

Sports version of the Mauser Parabellum in 7·65 mm Parabellum calibre with laterally flattened barrel.

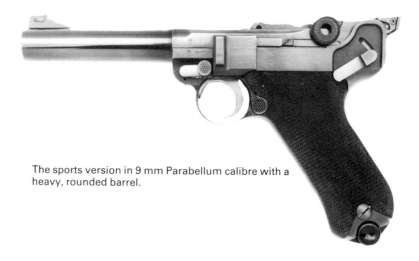

The sports version in 9 mm Parabellum calibre with a heavy, rounded barrel.

Various commemorative models

1975 Swiss model

Inscribed '75 Jahre Parabellum Pistole 1900-1975', on occasion of the anniversary of the adoption of this pistol by the Swiss Army. Calibre 7·65 mm Parabellum, barrel length 120 mm. Features the Swiss cross emblem surrounded by a halo on the receiver housing and engraved '·30 Luger' on top of the barrel and 'Original Mauser' on the toggle joint.

1977 Bulgarian model

Inscribed '75 Jahre Parabellum Pistole Königreich Bulgarien' (75 years Parabellum Pistol Kingdom of Bulgaria). Calibre 7·65 mm Parabellum, barrel length 120 mm. Features the Bulgarian coat of arms on the receiver housing and the intertwined emblem of DWM in gold on the front part of the toggle joint. The pistol has a protruding extractor on account of the adopted ammunition, and displays the word 'Loaded' in Cyrillic script, with the corresponding 'Safe' on safety. Contrary to the weapon depicted the inscriptions are not in white on the series-production pistols. Engraved on the barrel: '·30 Luger'.

1977 Russian model

Calibre 9 mm Parabellum, barrel length 100 mm. Inscribed on the left-hand side: '70 Jahre Parabellum Pistole Kaiserreich Russland' (70 years Parabellum Pistol Imperial Russia). In front of the receiver housing are two crossed Moisin-Nagant rifles and the intertwined emblem of DWM in gold on the front part of the toggle joint. On the extractor is the word 'Loaded', with the corresponding 'Safe' on safety in Cyrillic script. (Likewise not in white, on series-production pistols, unlike the weapon depicted.)

1979 German Navy

Calibre 9 mm Parabellum, barrel length 152 mm. The rear sight can be set for two distances. Inscribed on the side '75 Jahre Parabellum Pistole Kaiserliche Marine' (75 years Parabellum pistol Imperial (German) Navy). No engraving on the receiver housing, but has the intertwined DWM emblem in gold on the rear section of the toggle joint. On the butt there is a loop for a carrying strap and a milled attachment for the shoulder stock which unfortunately is not included. The pistol is delivered in a real leather case with raised stitching; there are two compartments: for the pistol, a magazine, box of ammunition and tools, and for the book *Luger* by John Walter in English inside the top cover.

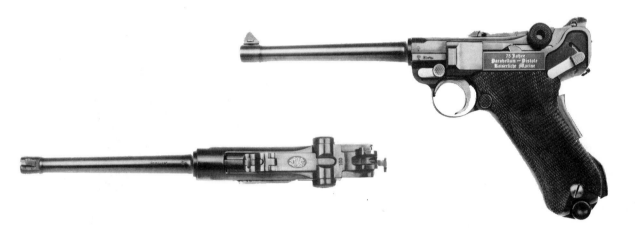

The Imperial German Navy model is delivered in a natural-colour leather case which accomodates the pistol, a spare magazine, tools, a box of ammunition and the book *Luger* by John Walter inside the top cover.

1980 Carbine

Calibre 9 mm Parabellum, barrel length 300 mm. Rounded, gradually narrowing barrel with a long cross-etched foresight ramp and a three-stage adjustable sliding sight that can be set for 100, 200 and 300 m ranges. No engraving on the receiver housing, but there is the DWM emblem in gold on the front part of the toggle joint. The butt has a milled attachment to fit the shoulder stock which, like the fore part of the wooden stock, is partially decorated with hand-carved 'fish-scale' pattern. The shoulder stock also has a sling swivel loop and a butt cover piece. Inscribed on the side: '75 Jahre Parabellum Pistole Mod. Karabiner'.

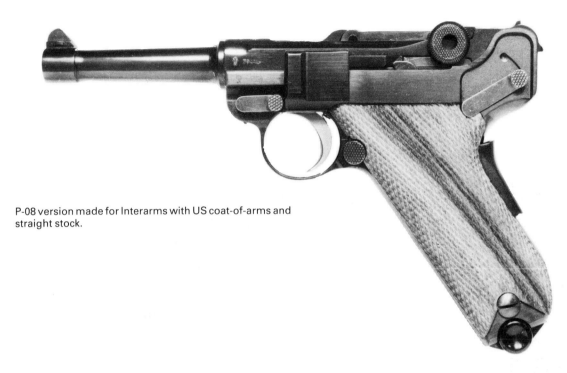

P-08 version made for Interarms with US coat-of-arms and
straight stock.

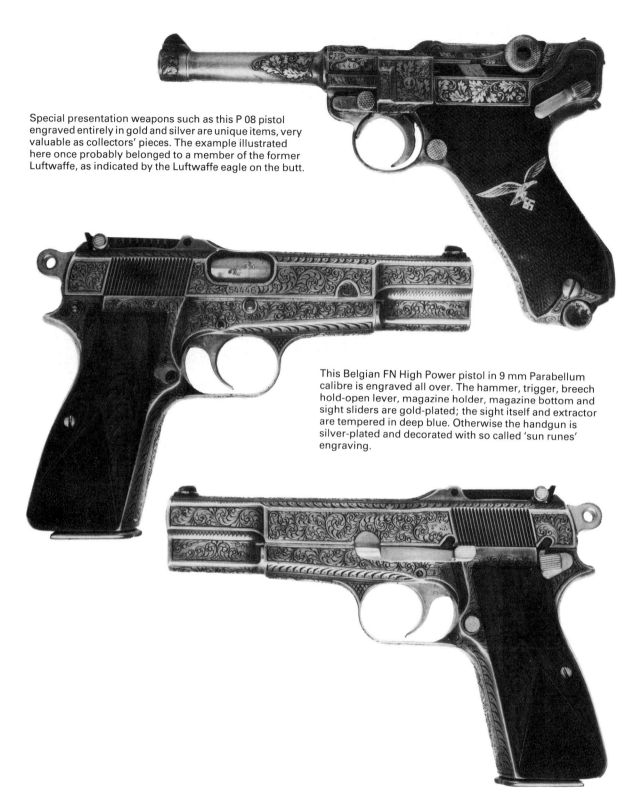

Special presentation weapons such as this P 08 pistol engraved entirely in gold and silver are unique items, very valuable as collectors' pieces. The example illustrated here once probably belonged to a member of the former Luftwaffe, as indicated by the Luftwaffe eagle on the butt.

This Belgian FN High Power pistol in 9 mm Parabellum calibre is engraved all over. The hammer, trigger, breech hold-open lever, magazine holder, magazine bottom and sight sliders are gold-plated; the sight itself and extractor are tempered in deep blue. Otherwise the handgun is silver-plated and decorated with so called 'sun runes' engraving.

An engraved Walther PPK pistol given as presentation weapon to an offical employed as the former State Security Main Office (RSHA).

Source Literature

BOCK, G. & WEIGEL, C. *Handbuch der Faustfeuer-waffen* (The Handbook of Handguns), 1974

ERLMEIER/BRANDT *Handbuch der Pistolen- und Revolverpatronen* (The Handbook of Pistol and Revolver Cartridges), Vols 1 and 2, 1967, 1980

EZELL, E. *Small Arms of the World*
Deutsches Waffenjournal (The German Weapons Journal) 1965-1982

HOGG, I. *Die deutschen Pistolen und Revolver 1871-1945* (German Pistols and Revolvers 1871-1945), Stuttgart, 1972

JINKS, R. *Smith & Wesson*, Stuttgart, 1979

KÖNIG, K. *Das Gross Buch der Faustfeuerwaffen* (The Big Book of Handguns), Stuttgart, 1980

MUSTER, H. *Revolver-Lexikon*, Stuttgart, 1978

MYATT, F. *Moderne Hand- und Faustfeuer-waffen, Maschinenwaffen und Panzerbüch-sen*, Stuttgart, 1980

PAWLAS, K. *Internationaler Waffen-Erken-nungsdienst* (International Weapons Recognition Service), Nürnberg

PAWLAS, K. *Pistolen-Atlas*, (Pistol Atlas), Nürnberg

PAWLAS K. *Waffen-Revue* (Weapons-Revue) issues 1-46, Nürnberg

RUTSCH, H. *Faustfeuerwaffen der Eidgenossen* (Handguns of the Swiss Confederation), Stuttgart, 1978

WALTER, J. *Luger* (English and German language editions), Stuttgart, 1982

Care and conservation

In addition to its rarity, the value of a collector's item is judged according to how close its present condition is to its original state immediately after manufacture. Often enough not much remains of this 'original condition', especially when it comes to military firearms that have been in service for several decades and not infrequently undergone some rough battering.

Usually the weapons offered to the collectors by the trade are classified as 'good', 'very good' and 'excellent'; the dealers readily charge a hefty price increase for that little bit of effort involved in selling a so-called 'selected item'. Often this price premium is quite a bit extra considering that all the dealer had to do was pick out reasonably well-preserved pieces from another surplus arsenal, the contents of which have been acquired at a knock-down price.

Much more accurate is the classification of condition and quality used by the well-known (German) firm of *Collector Guns* from whose current offers we have depicted quite a few handguns for inclusion in this volume. In this case the classification is according to American pattern and covers eleven grades:

1) new (mint)
2) near new (near mint)
3) very fine
4) fine
5) excellent
6) very good
7) good
8) quite good
9) fair
10) poor
11) relic

This classification provides a very good mental picture of the handgun concerned.

Once an item has been acquired the collector should concentrate all his efforts on handling, keeping and preserving the weapon so that its condition shows no perceptible change even after decades of storage or display. This applies especially to rust in visible or hidden parts.

Dismantling

The whole procedure begins with complete dismantling; depending on the owner's standard of knowledge it is advisable to take the weapon apart, down to its smallest screw. Those who are not quite sure of their subject should ask for advice. Hints regarding the dismantling of popular models can often be found in specialist literature, but there are times when the collector is faced by a seemingly insoluble problem, when it happens to be a handgun that does not seem to have been depicted or described anywhere. Thus for instance we needed almost half an hour to dismantle the Campo Giro pistol into its components and quite a bit longer to re-assemble it again. In the case of particularly difficult weapons it is advisable to make sketches and take notes, or photograph the individual stages of the dismantling process because the correct assembly is often more than just dismantling in reverse order.

Cleaning

It is only during the dismantling that the real condition of the weapon is revealed, and often enough the onset of rust and scratches spoil the overall picture.

As far as possible, all old and generally unpleasant-smelling, hardened grease and oil remains must be removed from the weapon. Care must be taken with chemical cleaning agents because one can never tell in advance how they will affect a gunmetal finish or make it blotchy. Instead of soaking such parts in various chemical thinners, turpentine or petroleum it is far better to boil them in water to which a few drops of Ballistol* have been added. This soon dissolves all grease, while rust undergoes a chemical change and is

* Ballistol and Schaft Oil are German proprietary brands for which equivalents exist in other countries. The advice of a gunsmith should be sought.

neutralized, turning into iron trioxide which produces a similar effect to bluing or gunmetal finish. In addition, the finely distributed drops of oil on the component parts drying in their own heat produce a protective film similar to the protective lacquer often contained in car-wash products.

The above-mentioned method of boiling in water can be successfully used for the bluing of smaller component parts, which then can be left to develop a light even layer of rust. The parts are then cooked in boiling water for about 20 mins, dried and rubbed all over with oil to protect them from further rusting.

Very little use should be made of steel brushes. Soft, thin-wired rotary brushes attached to an electric drill can be used to polish smooth parts, such as the slide on self-loading pistols. Only slight pressure should be applied to the parts being worked on and they should be treated until they are clean of all traces of rust. Parts that are polished with a rotary brush will never show the shine achieved with a piece of felt cloth and polishing paste. For this kind of work the trade offers a range of finely graded polishing pastes. Normally, a chromium polish will do the job, but if one would like to work even more carefully it is recommended to use car wax polish on a piece of felt.

Special care should be taken when cleaning ratchets and latches: an accidental 'rounding off' can easily destroy their function.

All smooth internal parts should always be well greased before reassembly. For this purpose it is best to use the colourless, scarcely noticeable gun vaseline.

Rust

If it did not exist, quite a few gun collectors would feel much better, because rust is the most frequently encountered problem.

We can only neutralize and prevent further spreading of rust on browned gunmetal parts. Deep scars left by rust can be got rid of by thorough grinding – which unfortunately also results in a somewhat altered weapon, and is therefore not recommended. Beginnings of a thick layer of rust can often be rubbed off with an oily rag; a more effective method is to use a piece of hard felt soaked in oil. Parts where this kind of thick rust has already gained solid hold can best be treated with the finest steel wool (Grade 000) that has been saturated with high-grade oil. Use it to rub the affected part carefully, stopping now and again to check the results.

Badly rusted parts, such as around the piston-area of muzzle loaders, can only be partially de-rusted. The most effective treatment is to use a circular brush attached to a drill, running it at high revs. This does not result in any visible scratches on the hard steel, and the finish is a matted silky shine.

Chemical de-rusting agents are not recommended because of their unpredictable effect on the existing surface. They can of course be used to treat deep-seated rust scars, but the actual effect of these chemicals hardly ever matches the claims made in advertisements.

Bluing

The existing condition of the original gunmetal finish is frequently part and parcel of the description of quality and has to be accepted as it is. Even a partial, never mind complete, rework of the metal bluing is a fundamental falsification of the original condition and results in an obligatory reduction of the price.

Despite all advertising, the commercially available 'cold bluing' is nowhere near as good as one is led to expect, apart from its use on smaller parts where this new 'gunmetal finish' will be seldom permanent in any case. No attempt should be made at all at 're-bluing' an older weapon, and one should not do any 'work' on imprints and engravings, for example. In this respect other standards and different reasoning have come into vogue in, for example, the USA.

Grip surfaces

As a rule, they only need a thorough cleaning to get rid of remains of grease and tallow. Here too it is advisable to take care. Furious cleaning methods, such as the use of oven cleaning sprays for example, will necessitate a re-grinding of the surface, which again is a falsification and reduces value.

The so-called 'fish scale' surfaces are best cleaned with a brand-new toothbrush, running it carefully in the direction of the grooves. Even the softest copper brush would be too hard for this task and could break out some of the small romboid-shaped pieces from the pattern. Using oil and brushing (with the toothbrush) at the same time remove most of even the deep-seated dirt without causing any damage. Flat wooden grip surfaces are cleaned with a piece of felt dipped into Schaft* oil, rubbing in a circular movement which will simultaneously clean, preserve and to some extent also polish the woodwork.

Cracks in the wooden grip surfaces can hardly be repaired with ordinary wood glue because the entire piece is usually saturated with oil. In such cases either the whole wooden grip surfaces or just the cracked or split area must be thoroughly washed with nitro thinner, repeating the process several times to draw out at least some of the oil. Small cracks can be quickly and almost invisibly repaired with one of the so-called 'instant adhesives'. These modern adhesives are based on acryl-cyanide which combines with airborn moisture and within a few minutes produces a transparent and durable connection that afterwards be safely smoothed down with some oil and the finest sandpaper.

Bad breaks in wood, and also grip surfaces in plastic and other synthetic material can be glued together with a twin-compound adhesive such as UHU-Plus Endfest 300. The join will be even more solid if the grip surfaces piece can be hardened in an oven for 15 minutes at 80°. After an hour or so it can then be smoothed down with a fine sandpaper.

*See footnote to page 257.

Leather

Hard and brittle or fragile leather can be made to regain some of its original elasticity by a prolonged and repeated rubbing with leather grease, leather oil or Ballistol. Good surface finish can be achieved by the repeated application of ordinary shoe polish, either neutral or coloured.

Ammunition and pistol holsters are best kept with some kind of 'filling', unless they are made to have a stable shape. The best 'filling' is not the handgun itself which would be affected by the tannic acids still remaining in the leather, but a packing of dry rags or screwed-up paper.

The storage of weapons

It must be ensured first and foremost that the weapons and their accessories and ammunition are stored according to relevant firearms rules and regulations. Some owners can keep their collections in a concreted room secured with an alarm system and display their treasures in such a way that they are revealed in all their beauty immediately the door is opened. However, often such collections have to be kept in secured rooms and inside locked cabinets, which in turn have to conform to appropriate legislation. One way or another, there will always be the problem of how best to display the collection of weapons – fix them in upright or horizontal position, or to hang them along the wall.

One of the best ways is to lay the weapons flat on a piece of felt, cloth or thin carpet underlay which has been stretched across an inlaid wooden framework fitted in the bottom of the cabinet. In my time I have seen rifles that have lost all their bluing and even developed considerable patches of rust on those sections of their barrels with which they had leaned against the velour lining in upright cabinets.

The underlaying support must be chemically neutral, particularly if it is glued to a piece of wood or metal. Instead of using an adhesive, the long-term effects of which cannot be foreseen, it is far better to stretch the piece of material or cloth across the framework, fastening it underneath.

Care must be taken if the weapons are kept for long periods of time inside locked strong-boxes. Only a short while ago, while checking the Mauser 'Jubilee'-pistols in my collection, I discovered considerable patches of rust near some of their safety catches. It came off with a brass brush and some Ballistol but it served as a warning.

In my experience simple wooden supports are the best. The bottom inlay consists of pieces of board that have been glued together in several layers and then saturated with oil. To date, even after prolonged storage in a not yet quite dried out cellar I have not noticed any unfavourable side effects such as rust or any discoloration of bluing.

Care of the weapons

It is not necessary constantly to clean and oil the guns in a collection, but a regular check-up of all the items is advisable.

Fingerprints can be especially unpleasant, particularly if the collection is kept in an unsuitable cellar: over a period of time, the acids in human sweat always present at the finger tips are guaranteed to have an adverse effect on the gunmetal browning. Some collectors rub their hands with high-grade oil before picking up or replacing the guns in their collections. An even more effective way is to wear a pair of thin cloth gloves and offer the same to any visitors.

The cabinets

The better-known firms supplying collectors' guns now also offer a wide selection of steel cabinets for shorter or longer items, all of which comply with the current safety rules and regulations regarding the keeping of firearms.

This poses a problem to a collector of handguns who would like to acquire and store as many items as he possibly can – for which the available cabinets, designed mainly for the storage of rifles, are hardly suitable.

However, a cabinet to safely store a large number of handguns can also be obtained elsewhere. Other very suitable storage containers are the steel cabinets with wide, deep drawers used by architects for their large-format drawings.

Tools

It is not really necessary to have many tools: a good set of screwdrivers of various sizes is the most important. However, here one always has to ensure that the width of the screwdriver blade completely fills the slit on the screw-head both in depth and width.

For further dismantling it is also necessary to have a set of drift punches. The best are those with a casing which lets the punch slide through without any play.

It is advisable to have a plastic hammer because there are times when a certain amount of gentle force is needed in dismantling a handgun.

Other 'special' tools are seldom required; after all, the average gun collector is probably 'technical' enough to have a well-stocked home workshop.

Acknowledgements

In the acquisition of this comprehensive illustrated material we were greatly helped by numerous private collectors to whom we would like to express our sincerest thanks. A very special 'thank you' is due to the firm of *Collector Guns* at Altenkirchen who kindly allowed us to photograph many rare and difficult-to-obtain collectors' items from their stock.

The authors